# Home
# When the
# Streetlights
# Come On

MR. HANK J LEO JR.

ISBN: 1479206229
ISBN 13: 9781479206223

*"Hank Leo's stories about life are as simple, innocent, and powerful as the visions of Charles Schultz and Fred Rogers. On a bad day, Hank makes me smile and recognize again what I still like about life. For sheer laughs, 'The Car Wash' is pure Lucille Ball, a timeless classic."*

**JENNIFER WARNES, OSCAR & GRAMMY AWARD WINNING ARTIST**

*"My friend Hank has dedicated his life to giving to others so that their lives may be enriched. Here's yet another gift from Hank for all, humorous, witty, and rich with life's little adventures."*

**MITCH PLAYER, PROFESSIONAL MUSICIAN, PRESERVATION HALL, NEW ORLEANS**

*"Hank Leo is a man whose thoughtfulness, grace, and humanity are a lighthouse in a sea of sometimes seeming darkness. I am always pleased and comforted to hear his voice, as I shake his hand, on the phone, or on the printed page. He reminds me there is hope. Enjoy!"*

**BRIAN O'NEAL, FOUNDER, LEAD SINGER FOR THE BUSBOYS**

*"I totally loved reading these stories by Hank Leo, a caring and considerate person who brilliantly weaves treasured stories you will want to read!"*

**JOANNE SHENANDOAH, AUTHOR, GRAMMY-WINNER RECORDING ARTIST**

*"As a newspaper editor I often receive samples from aspiring columnists, and they're frequently quite good. Over the years I've learned most people have a good column or two or three in them, but few have more than that. Hank Leo's been writing his weekly column now for nearly two years and his take on life continues to be fresh, interesting, and varied."*

**KURT WANFRIED, EDITOR, *ONEIDA DAILY DISPATCH***

# Prologue

*At the urging of many neighbors, friends, and community members, I was encouraged to compile a book of the weekly articles I have submitted to the* Oneida Daily Dispatch *over the years about my crazy adventures and daily living in a small town. When I was searching for publishing companies to print my book, there were plenty of warnings provided to first-time authors:*

*First, do not write about personal experiences. The only people that will read the book are your family members and friends to make you feel good and that's not a guarantee, either.*

*Second, do not write about small towns. The audience is small, just like the town, and it will only appeal to locals.*

*Third, do not get your high school English teacher to help you or to edit your work for you.*

*And fourth, do not write a prologue. No one reads them.*

*With that said, this is a book about my personal weekly adventures, living in Oneida, New York, a small city of 11,000 people. I hope to reach many people, all outside of a one-mile radius of Oneida, not just my family and friends. My high school English teacher, Debra Longnecker, helped me through the revision process. And finally, this is a prologue and you are reading it.*

# Game's Over – Time to Go Home

If "Home is where the heart is," my heart can be found in Oneida, New York, at Allen Park where I spent hour after hour with my friends, playing and learning. Today when I drive by, I wish I could stop and talk to the families who live there now. I'd like to tell them that the Park has a wonderful story to tell. It's filled with love, laughter, friendship, and adolescence, all illuminated by one old streetlight.

When I was a kid, we were pretty much free to do anything or go anywhere in the neighborhood, as long as we were home before dark. I would always yell on my way out the door, "Mom, going to Tommy's house!" without even waiting for a reply. Mom would always remind me, "As long as you make sure you're home when the streetlights come on!" She didn't even know which Tommy I was referring to or where he lived. But there was trust in the neighborhood and families took care of each other.

There weren't the worries then that there are today. I don't recall any discussions of drug pushers approaching us kids. I don't recall anyone acting crazy on bath salts. I certainly don't remember ever feeling my life was in jeopardy. I think if anyone was on bath salts and trying to harm us, he or she would have their hands full. Twenty-five to thirty kids would have prevented that.

I lived across the street from Allen Park. It was my second home. I spent most of my childhood shooting baskets on a wooden backboard with broken boards. Grass was growing up through the asphalt. The Park Clubhouse was our "fort" and the baseball or kickball game was played on a set of trees made for first and third base. Second was someone's shirt and home was someone's hat. All we needed was a ball. The trees made for great Hide and Seek or games of tag. The tennis courts doubled as a stadium. The streetlight closest to my house was home base for Kick-the-Can. Kids would run all over the park after the can was kicked and one team had to tag all of the members of the other team and put them at the home spot. If you got all of them tagged at home, the game was over.

Streetlights coming on served as both a sign the game was over and as a signal to head home. Mine was easy, as I just walked across the street. Others had to walk around the block to their houses. No video games, no television. We were tired and ready for bed. I don't recall too many overweight or bored kids in my neighborhood. Running, playing, planning, organizing, and participating happened naturally and freely. There wasn't any adult intervention or supervision. We didn't need it and we wouldn't have accepted it.

Every time I see the streetlights come on now, I am reminded of a simpler time. Today, those lights don't mean "game over." They do, however, remind me to head home. Reflecting on those times and all the times between then and now allow me to do just that.

# Don't Be in Such a Hurry to Grow Old...

It seems that when we are in our teens, we just can't wait to grow up and get a car, find a job, buy a house, and travel. When we get older, we wish we didn't have all of those responsibilities. The car needs gas, oil changes, tires, and brakes. The job eliminates at least 40 hours a week of our fun time and the house costs way more than we thought it would. Traveling happens once the other three are paid. I was thinking over the weekend about what we used to do for fun as kids and came up with my list of memories.

I actually did have a Slinky. I started it at the top of the stairs; it got caught on the third step every time, and stopped right there. I always had to run up the stairs to get it started again. Games were equally frustrating. I never really understood the theory behind Trouble, the board game. I guess they figured when kids rolled dice they always fell on the floor, so they put a bubble over it. We did play Old Maid. Wow, was she ugly. No wonder why no one wanted to get her card. My dad had an old picture of a lady from high school that looked just like her. He used to show it to us as kids and tell us it was his first girlfriend. We wondered why he dated the ugliest lady in a card deck, and how he eventually courted mom, given this knowledge.

My little sister had a Holly Hobby Gazebo. I used to put our cat in it and sail it down the stairs to see if she was dizzy when she came out. It worked. I also had Rock 'em Sock 'em Robots. You hit the other boxer robot under the chin and his head popped up. I had an Etch-A-Sketch. I used to try like crazy to make a circle with it by using both hands. Never happened. The whole family played Monopoly and got pizza from Pepi's, our local pizza dynasty. I remember thinking, "Wow, look at all of this money I have. Three hundred bucks!" Now, ironically, that's my monthly car payment.

I used to watch the Waltons. I think I shed a tear during the Homecoming episode (the Christmas one), where John Boy went looking for his father. I loved my record player. We used to collect 45s. I can't tell you how strange it was when they replaced the little spiral inserts used to position the record on the turntable with the solid circular ones. I thought, "What took them so long to invent a solid one?" Sometimes if you lost the insert, you tried to eyeball it and see if you could get it in the middle. All that did was make Tony Orlando's "Knock Three Times" sound like K.N.N.N.O.O.O.C.K. T.H.H.H.R.R.R.E.E.E. T.I.I.I.M.E.S.S.S.S."

My dad had a CB in his station wagon. It was cool to learn all of the trucker terms and handles. "This is Hurricane Hank comin' up on yer tail; catchya on the flipside; we gone. Bye bye." Tuesday nights was *Happy Days* and *Laverne & Shirley*, in that order. I always wondered what would have happened if the Six Million Dollar Man and the Bionic Woman had children. I wanted to be that kid. My dad and I got up every Sunday morning and watched Abbott & Costello, laughing like crazy, especially at the "Invisible Man" episode. Sometimes we watched *Maude* (She may have been the model they used to create the Old Maid) and *The Courtship of Eddie's Father.* The widower was, of course, Bill Bixby, who went on to become the Incredible Hulk. And watching Carl Kolchak find vampires in "The Night Stalker" scared the b'jeepers out of me.

I learned how to swim in our neighbor's pool. Dad threw in a dollar and that was motivation enough. I came up choking and gasping for air, but a dollar richer. Now I'm in charge of an organization that teaches kids to swim. We had a tree house. Dad built it and it was great. Now it serves as a place to hang the grill utensils when we have cookouts. The summer game was Jarts.

Not "lawn darts," but "JARTS." They were sharp, made of steel, and you tossed them into a plastic ring on the lawn. Now I look back and think about how I could have been walking around with a Jart in my sneaker or my eye. We played "Mother May I?" and "Red Light, Green Light." I can't remember the rules other than it taught me to ask my mom permission for everything, even to this day. My sisters could all do the "Cat's Cradle" with a piece of yarn. Later, in school, a piece of paper turned out to be the thing that determined who you were going to marry by the way it was folded up. Using finger movements and counting your favorite number yielded answers written on the insides of the flaps. Sometimes mine determined that I was marrying Mike Johnson, which always brought laughter from the girl carrying out the exercise.

So...don't be in such a hurry to grow old. Get out and play. This morning, as I came up the YMCA sidewalk, I saw the kids had chalked a hopscotch course. With briefcase in one hand and coffee in the other, I did the whole thing. Don't know if anyone saw me, but it didn't really matter. I just smiled, came in, sat at my computer, and typed this.

# Who are "They" Anyway?

Yesterday, I believe I heard on multiple occasions, "You know what they say..." and I wondered just who "they" are. The first one was, "They say it's supposed to clear up later." I am assuming on this occasion the reference is to a collective group of weather professionals, sort of like a collage of meteorologists whom everyone seems to watch at different times and puts together in their minds as a knowledgeable group. No one ever really knows if "they" are correct, but if you quote them, it must have some credibility because someone other than you said it. No one ever questions the validity of "they" either.

"They say eggs are bad for you," went through numerous challenges. "They" first probably referred to the doctors. "They" then may have switched to the grocery stores. "They" then could have meant the farmers, contradicting the doctors. Now when you use "they" in regard to eggs, you have to be careful because it has changed so much we aren't sure whom to believe anymore. "They" could be the chickens themselves, for all I know.

"You know what they say; the more the merrier." This is most often true. Party planners, concert promoters, festival organizers want to be the collective "they." This should not apply to let's say, funeral directors or waste managers. Or, how about "You know what they say; you can't take it with you." Now here, "they" has to refer to the dearly departed, sitting at the pearly gates, apparently checking baggage. "You know what they say; you get what you pay for," must refer to a group of accountants. Only this group would want to verify the number of peanut M&Ms you just bought.

"You know what they say; you can't have it both ways," most likely was not compiled by a group of chefs. This group prides itself on giving you Eggs Benedict, scrambled, poached, over-easy, or hard-boiled. And they can mix and match. "Absolutely, you can have it both ways," the cooks would say. "You can't have your cake and eat it too," was not said by a chef, though. Imagine birthday parties if they were right.

"You know what they say; when you've seen one, you've seen them all." Try telling this to an astronomer or a dating service. "They don't make 'em like they used to," is a tough one. Houses come to mind, followed by cars. But phones? I can't imagine having a cord or antenna anymore.

I am not altogether sure if there is a group of scholars, doctors, lawyers, accountants, mathematicians, and meteorologists that sit in one room and brainstorm sayings. It is possible, I guess. I am amazed by the credibility we give the current group of "theys" without even knowing "they" exist. Maybe I could start a local company, call it "Us," and have people ask a whole bunch of common questions and we give people our philosophical answers with some credence. Just an idea. "If you need an opinion to prove a point, just call US and we'll give you one," might be our motto. Then you can say with confidence, "You know what they say; if it's not one thing, it's another."

Well, "You know what they say; long speeches and columns make for short friendships." So I will end here.

# Sleeping as an Art Form

I still haven't mastered it. Every night, it's pretty much the same routine: brush my teeth, turn on the TV or read a book, lights out, and attempt to find la la land. I always envy those people who can just put their head on the pillow and they are out, waking up eight or so hours later. Thunderstorms don't bother them. Rain doesn't bother them. There could be a bomb going off in the bedroom and these folks just don't move. Not me.

First, it takes me several attempts to get comfortable. On my left, on my right, on my back, then the front. It's not restless leg syndrome; it's restless body syndrome. There have been times I have fallen asleep on one arm, only to wake up and think I'm being hugged by a corpse. The arm is completely numb and I could pinch it without feeling a thing. Other times I wake up and can't breathe through my nose at all and there are drool marks on the pillow. I've tried counting sheep, but I lose my place and have to start all over again.

Eventually, I presumed I had a sleep disorder, and went to a sleep clinic to have myself tested. I guess I was correct because I think I recorded 275 "episodes" during the night. I was rigged with the C-Pap machine to open the airways and correct any of the dysfunctions I might have had. The only thing it did for me was scare the heck out of me when I got up one night to use the bathroom, looked in the mirror, and thought I was Darth Vader. I almost took out my toothbrush and tried to use it as a light saber. Others swear by it, and rightfully so. More oxygen, more sleep.

I also usually hog the bed, rolling from one side to another, then to the middle. The littlest thing will wake me up. I can hear a cricket chirping from thirty miles away. And a neighbor's barking dog might as well be sitting on the bed right next to my ear. Sometimes I wake up and I can't turn my neck left or right. People think I am rude when they say hi and I stare straight ahead, not acknowledging them. I'm also pretty sure I snore. No, I am sure, because I have awakened myself on more than one occasion with a loud gurgling sound, thinking the Monday morning garbage truck had come early. I'm surprised the curtains weren't in my mouth.

I am envious of those who can take power naps. Some people just sit down in a chair and they fall soundly asleep for twenty minutes, wake up, and feel refreshed and ready to go. If I sleep for twenty minutes, I feel like I'm stuck in a dream, not sure what day or time it is, and I have to check the morning paper to see if the current events are current. I've even started making breakfast at 7 PM after one of these things. One time, I tried to take a "sleep-aid" to fall asleep. This just made me feel like a zombie for the next two days and caused everyone to ask me if I had been in a bus accident.

Recently, I figured out what to do to improve my evening rest. I turn on some light piano music, you know, the new-age stuff. I wake up the next day, fully rested, but humming "Evening Waterfalls" all day long.

# Mommy and Me

For the last eight or so months, I have had the pleasure of working alongside one of my employees at the YMCA, Stephanie. Stephanie is about ready to have her first baby. This is the first time in my life I have ever been around a pregnant woman day-by-day during the entire span and I have learned much just by being there. Remember, at work you are with people for at least eight hours a day, so you get to see and know people very well.

I always ask Stephanie if she is excited or nervous and she always says, "Excited!" I am nervous. I have watched her grow, both professionally and, well, you know. I always tell her to let me know when the first signs of anything even remotely close to a kick, squirm, or discomfort happens, so I can hurry up and boil water, then go into shock. I have thought about running into the steam room and hiding. I tell her not to bend over to pick up a paper clip, and to let me handle anything even close to physical labor, and I warn her to "be careful" hundreds of times a day. I get scared when she puts up a poster. I always kid with her that there had better be plenty of others around if this baby decides it wants to enter the world at the Y when I happen to be Director on Duty.

Stephanie most always says, "I can't wait to see her, be with her, and love her." She has shown me ultrasound photos that I have held upside down while remarking "Wow, she's beautiful," and Stephanie calmly turns the picture and empathetically replies, "No, this way-that's her feet, not her head." Who am I to tell? It looked like a nose. The other day, I saw how truly happy and eager a young mom is, waiting to have her first-born baby in her arms, ready to accept the child into the world. It made me understand why so many mothers, all of them I would imagine, nurture, protect, defend, and love their babies unconditionally. They would die for them. The love starts the minute they know they are pregnant and never subsides. I can see it. This isn't much of an epiphany to all of you that have children- you've "gotten it" for thousands of years. For a guy like me, it took awhile, and it is beautiful to watch and experience.

So I follow Stephanie around with the defibrillators, band aids, ice packs, duct tape (there must be some use for that in this somewhere), scissors, scotch tape, and calculator, not knowing if any of these are needed, but that's all we have in the office. I may bring some colored paper and the manila folders for good measure. I guess if there is a need for a collage, I am ready to roll. I'm not sure I'll need the laminator either, but it is an arm's length away, just in case. We have walkie-talkies but I'm confused about what the maintenance guy would do if I paged him; probably no more help than I. She just looks at me like I'm crazy and says not to worry. I worry. She says I am more worried than her husband. I am. She says, "Hank, women have been having babies for thousands of years." I reply, "Not in the Y when I'm Director on Duty." If I hear her yell, or say, "It's time!" I'll probably instinctively close the pool, for no apparent reason other than that's what we do. We call our blue emergency buttons "panic buttons." I have already hit them four or five times and when the staff come running, I reason, "Sorry, I was just doing a drill on myself."

I want to thank Stephanie for teaching me the ways of the world, motherhood, the miracle of life on its way, and forgiving me for being an overprotective supervisor. I also want to thank her for forgiving me for my lack of "dad-knowledge." If she has the baby at the Y, I am ready, stapler and file folders in hand.

# Junk Drawers

Everyone has them. They are always in the kitchen, next to the stove or sink somewhere. They are always overstuffed, in random order, and you aren't sure why you put things in them or why you are saving the items. The other day I went through mine to determine whether to keep or toss. Here are the results, in no particular order:

Paper Clips. These metal marvels are everywhere in various sizes and colors, but when bored, I unbend them, wrap them around my finger, they fall on the floor and for some reason, vacuum cleaners struggle to pick them up. They rattle for a few seconds then get spit back out on the floor. I'm not sure whether or not to throw them in the garbage or the recycling bin. They stay in the drawer.

Pennies. Nothing costs a penny anymore, and we leave them as tips. Cashiers always have extra ones to make the bill work out evenly. You need a hundred of them to make it even worthwhile to save them. For that matter, nothing costs a dollar anymore either. They stay in the drawer.

Canadian Pennies. See above, only more worthless.

Keys. I have dozens of keys. I am not sure at all what they lock or unlock. I think I have keys from four cars ago, three houses ago, six apartments ago, and two bike locks. I'm afraid to throw them away in case I come across something I can't open and need a key. They stay, but reluctantly.

Pictures of Non-Important Stuff. I have photos of birds, frogs, a tree, a mouse, a giraffe, a stool, a leaf, and a rock. I am not sure why, but assume they were taken during a vacation or some time when I thought something was cool for a minute and took the picture. I would never put them in an album, and would have a hard time discussing their significance to anyone. They could go.

Cords. I have plugs and cords that number in the hundreds. One end plugs into the wall, the other plugs into who knows what. They might be cords for phones, Walk-Men, cassette players, and more. All of the cords are tangled and in the back. The interesting thing is that there are no phones, Walk-Men, or cassette players to be found, only these cords. Apparently I am waiting for their safe return home. Just when I dispose of them, I will inevitably need one. They stay.

Batteries. Plenty of them, all voltages. I have a 9V, a D, two Cs, a bunch of AAs, and eighteen AAAs. None of them works. I'm not even sure where to discard them. They stay, because no junk drawer should be without them.

A Hammer. I have a tool chest in the basement, and one in the garage, but it is always handy to have a hammer near the kitchen. I don't know why, but it stays.

Pot Holders. There are six of them and I only have two hands. They don't match the décor of any of the rooms. They stay.

Pens That Don't Work. Literally, there are sixteen pens and none of them writes. I scribble something on a scrap paper (from the junk drawer, of course), find out they don't work, and throw them back in the junk drawer. I might need them someday to poke a hole through something. They stay.

Pencils with Broken Lead. Three of these grace the drawer. They stay, only because I might find a sharpener by the end of this writing.

A Thimble. I think I forgot what thimbles are for. It doesn't fit any of my fingers and I would have to call Mom to have her explain it to me. It stays until I know what it does again.

Phone Book from 2003 with Torn Cover. It takes up a lot of room and sits on top of the mound, making the drawer a challenge to close every time. It obviously does not list cell phone numbers and no one uses house phones anymore. It stays for the sole purpose of supporting the scrap paper to see if the pens write.

Birthday Card from "Jan." I have no idea who Jan is, or why I saved this card. It's not very sentimental and it was under the phone book. It's not even personalized; it only says "Happy Belated Birthday, Jan." It stays until I figure out who she is.

Film Rolls. I am not even sure whom to bring these to or if I want to know what is on them. If they were important, I would have had them developed, I think. They were in the way back, possibly for a good reason. They stay, out of sheer intrigue.

Tootsie Rolls. Two of them, near the front. I am not sure of the longevity or shelf life of a Tootsie Roll. There is no "Born on" date. They are traditionally hard anyway, so it would be difficult to determine age. They stay.

A Spring. It looks like the spring from a pen, but it is just a spring. I squeezed it a couple of times and it still works. Of course, I could squeeze it and let it fly across the room, but I would find it again and place it back in the junk drawer. It stays because of this possibility.

Various Forms of Tape. I have Scotch, painters, electrical, double-sided and a tape measure. Tape never seems to get old. These rolls could be decades old, but they still stick reasonably well. They stay.

Baseball Card of Ed Armbrister. He played for the Cincinnati Reds, and wasn't all that great. I'm not sure why I kept the card. It's bent and you can barely make out the stats on the back from the gum stains. I don't particularly like the card, but his name is interesting. It stays.

Wooden Ruler with the Inch Numbers Worn Off. I have a tape measure, making this obsolete, but one always needs a straight edge for something. It stays.

Bookmark. Or, at least I think it is a bookmark. It's flat, has no writing on it, and could be used as one. It stays.

Scrap Paper with "228-4386" on it. Of course this is something I need to dial, to find out who it is. I'm just not sure what I would say. "Hi, you were in my junk drawer. Do you know why?" I can't bring myself to do it. Then again, it might not be a number and could be a combination to one of the padlocks stored randomly in the right-hand side of the drawer. It stays, to keep the mystery alive.

The odd thing is that even after evaluating the importance of my drawer, going through the "keep or ditch" decisions, it remains the same. Maybe I'll check it again in a year or two.

# Then and Now

Whenever entering the first week of a new year, I am reminded of some differences between when we were growing up "back in the day" and now. So much has changed. I'll refer to "then" as my childhood and "now" as this year. Here we go…

Then, I was told to stick my face in a book; now, the first thing I check in the morning is my Facebook.

Then, I was playing baseball with 17 of my friends; now, I am drinking Chai Tea after I take Tai Chi.

Then, I thought wine was something old women drank; now, I have a wine rack, wine glasses, and wine charms- and I've been on two wine tours.

Then, I would walk from home to the bus station for a comic book; now, I have to take a rest stop when walking the dog around the block.

Then, we had UHF and only got channels 3, 5, and 9; now, we have a 46-inch, hi-def, flat screen that gets 972 channels and I only watch 3, 5, and 9.

Then, a cell phone was what a prisoner used to get for his one call; now, everyone has one except the prisoner.

Then, a video game was Frogger or Pacman; now, you can be Derek Jeter with the bases loaded in the ninth.

Then, it was essential you learned to write and type; now, texting has Webster rolling around in his grave. LOL.

Then, homes were made out of wood and steel; now, my house moves when the wind blows.

Then, NYC was a once-in-a lifetime trip; now, it is a once-a-year trip. I drive 300 miles annually to watch the Mets lose.

Then, all food was made from scratch; now, scratching is what I do after I eat processed food.

Then, my car lasted ten years; now, my loan lasts much longer than the car.

# Man's Best Friend

I must confess that I am one of those fools who actually believes his dog is part human, despite the claims of professionals and non-dog lovers. Dogs have long been a part of our family, and the older I get, the more I realize they are a part of others, as well. Recently, I came home to find my Siberian Husky noticeably limping and yelping. He was in pain, and so was I. I took him to the vet, where they found he had a back problem and I was advised to take him home. He's an older dog and I wasn't sure what to do. After carrying him up the steps and helping him to his food bowl, I put a blanket down on the floor and laid him down. He put his head on my lap and we both had a good cry. I prayed out loud for God to help him, and reminded Him of how much Louie means to me. It isn't surprising to understand that dog is spelled God backwards. We walk together, talk together (yes, Huskies talk), and play together. Lonely, you say? Maybe, but fortunate is how I feel.

Those who are dog lovers know just what dogs are: best friends, confidants, companions, exercise mates, and in some ways, children. They are non-judgmental and accepting. They seem to understand the term "unconditional love" better than many humans. When you have a dog in your family for 15, 16, 17 years, he becomes an actual part of the family. Dog owners know the down-side. They destroy things, they chew things, they eat things they're not supposed to, they make mistakes. They get sick, they have accidents, they chase the mailman, they get loose and run off. On the other hand, they are loyal. They can sense fear, sadness, agitation, and happiness. They protect their families. There are stories of amazing rescues and sacrifices for their owners, even strangers. I have been upset over a death of someone I know and my dog was well aware of it and did his best to make me feel better. I have talked to dozens of others who feel the same way. They tell me that when they've gone through a rough stretch, their dog is the first thing they want to see and be with when they get home. Dogs know. If you ever want to see a face light up, or a story unfold, or a guard let down, ask even the stodgiest of people, or the most prominent business person in your circle. They will tell you a story of their family's first pet and share a great memory. I've hugged people who have lost their dog; I understand and I've cried with them. There have been times for me, just as I am sure for many others, when I have had a tough day. Just as I am about to vent my frustration, Louie will come and lick my face, or knock over a vase…it depends on the day. The troubles don't seem to last much longer after the laughter.

To the many of you out there that have a special family pal, or another pet that is an important part of you and your life every day, cheers to you for taking good care of them and recognizing their value. As Ben Williams once said, "There is no psychiatrist in the world like a puppy licking your face."

# Bible Study I

I was advised never to write about religion or politics...well, I apologize in advance. I went to Sunday school as a kid, and went to church sporadically throughout my adulthood. It wasn't until last year that I started reading the Bible before I go to bed every night. I started out with the traditional hotel nightstand version, but couldn't understand it at all. I was embarrassed that it seemed like so many great people quoted verses and I couldn't even understand the first page. The "thys," "begats," "covenants," and other terms were confusing and hard for me to translate. I bought a pocket dictionary or used Wikipedia on my cell phone just to figure out context. I had questions...Why do we say "God Bless You" when someone sneezes? Is this where we get the term "Doubting Thomas"? Does God look like Charlton Heston? The most interesting was finding the lyrics to the Byrd's "Turn, Turn, Turn" in there. Someone suggested I get a Study Bible. I did, then read "The Message," "The Story," and "The Voice." I read "The Prophet," a bunch of others, and finally, "Blue Like Jazz," which was more my speed. It takes me six books to get what many others get in one because I am a slow reader. If Dr. Seuss had written a translation, I would have purchased the first copy.

Now that I get it, it means a lot to me. I am developing a relationship with God, and it's a strong and beautiful one. I find it odd now that many people think things shouldn't be talked about and this topic in particular scares people. It shouldn't. When devil movies come out, everyone talks about them; when something good is discovered, it sometimes gets lost in the shuffle.

It took me a long time. Slow learner, maybe. Here's my summary of what I now understand that I am supposed to do and at close to 50 years old, I wish I'd started sooner: Be nice to people and care about them even though they might not be nice to me or even know who I am; Mean what I say and say what I mean; Spread happiness; Don't be afraid of the sick, the poor, the ones who don't have what you have - they are going to be first in line. In fact, give them what is most important: dignity. There's only one who's perfect, and it isn't me. Love and listen to my mom and dad. Love my neighbors and that doesn't just mean the people next door. And the most important lesson I learned: Everyone waits until there is a tragedy to pray. I believe you can't pray just to have great things happen to you. We shouldn't only pray for miracles. I don't think it works that way. I think I have to believe first, and miracles happen because I believe. Proof is everywhere.

What I have learned shouldn't be a secret. It's not a gift, either. I've never been what some call a "holy roller" or someone who preaches the Gospel. I don't even know it very well yet. I can't quote psalms or verses; I'm not even sure I'd be qualified to do so. I read them, try to understand them. When I finally think I've made sense of one, I just try to apply it to what I can do better. I try to live close to the way I understand it. I always thought life should come with an instruction manual. I am pleased to have found one. I stumble along the way all the time. I ask for forgiveness for my stupidity. I try to apply what I'm learning to my life. I also made a promise to myself that I would be a better friend, better brother, better son, and better member of my community. I try to listen twice as much as I talk. I want to be less selfish, more available to people who might need me. I don't want to pass judgment on others, nor am I qualified to preach how to be or how to live. I'm still working on me and have a long, long way to go. But I do understand that hope lifts spirits and it is free to give.

Something to leave you with that I read tonight: "Give ear to my words, consider my sighing" (Psalm 5:1). There's more of course, but, the message, I think, is that we should listen to people when they need us. We should pay attention to the needs around us and respond with care and compassion. We should care just as we would want to be cared for, and sighs are as important as words. Just listen.

# The Definition of True Happiness

True Happiness is...

- Taking clothes out of the dryer and finding $20 in a pocket

- A fudgie on a hot Sunday afternoon

- Catching a tailwind on your flight home

- Finding out cancer lost the battle, not you

- Rubbing away the crusties when you wake up

- Still finding crayons interesting

- That lady who lets you in front of her because you only have a few items

- Finding out your cholesterol is lower than your IQ

- Thunderstorms from the porch

- A fireplace in the winter

- A fire pit in the summer

- Corn on the cob in August

- Vanilla ice cream on top of a crushed Oreo, with chocolate syrup

- Leaning back in the chair and catching yourself just in time

- Getting a haircut in the middle of a heat wave

- Long weekends

- Cannonballs in the pool

- Dryfit anything

- Finding a coupon for a Buy One, Get One Free anything

- A ballgame, hotdog, peanuts, and Crackerjacks

- Cool Ranch Doritos

- Boxers...both the dogs and the undergarments

# Drains and Fountains

Last weekend, I visited my friend in Connecticut. On the way, I heard the DJ on the radio reference a quote that "People are either fountains or drains." I didn't think too much about it until I got home on Sunday. All I could think about is how true that is - that there are givers and takers in the world. To some extent, we are all a little of both.

As we get older, we tend to reflect on life. When you're younger, you just kind of live and go through things quickly. When you get older, you start to reminisce: What could I have done differently? Have I done more good than harm? How will I be remembered? I think I used to be a drain; I'm sure I was on some people. How many times did I take instead of give? How much help did I want and how much did I give someone who needed it more than I? How many times did I turn the other way when someone needed my help? A drain.

Drains suck the energy from others. These are the people who are angry all the time, complain about everything, always feel like they've gotten the short end of the stick. They are never happy. They are the ones who hate the weather, but never move. They are the ones who think they always have bad luck, but do nothing to reverse things. They are the ones who step in dog poop and blame it on the dog. We all know drains.

Fountains always seem to be happy and make those around them happy. They give, and don't expect anything in return. They seem to spurt life without ever letting you know they are tired or don't feel like spurting any more. Fountains make everyone around them feel better. They are the ones drains go to for more water. Fountains give forth, whether it's encouragement, help, happiness, or fun. Everybody knows a fountain. My mom is one of the best fountains I know.

Things get stuck in drains.
Kids like to play in fountains.

Drains get clogged with stuff.
Fountains create rainbows.

Drains need chemicals to release their problems.
Fountains need someone to turn them on.

Drains sink.
Fountains rise.

Drains need someone to fix them when they break.
Fountains just need someone to watch them perform.

Drains, like snakes, are earthbound.
Fountains, like birds, reach for the sky.

Drains tend to lose people's wishes
Fountains make wishes come true.

I want to be a fountain. And it's not that hard to make the choice every day.

# The Emergency Room

It was a frigid Saturday evening in upstate New York and I was driving home from a gathering at a friend's house, when suddenly the car in front of me skidded abruptly and spun a complete circle in the middle of the highway. That "black ice" that Central New Yorkers know all too well was glaring through the gigantic snow-flakes that looked like baseballs coming at me in 3-D on the wind-shield. As I swerved out of the way to the passing lane to avoid the car, mine spun out of control as well and hit a guardrail. There was some damage to the car and I was okay, but the car was in a ditch and I wasn't sure if I had broken anything, was in shock, or just scared to death- probably all three.

The ambulance arrived and took me away, just for precaution-ary measures; of course the other car was fine and continued on. When I arrived at the hospital, I went into the emergency room and sat and waited. And waited. Since I wasn't in any immediate danger, and since it was almost 11:30 PM, I was pretty content to just be alive, and sat patiently in the chair, staring at the TV. Just then, the electric doors opened and in came a woman pushing an elderly gentleman in a wheelchair. He was clasping his arms tightly against his stomach, where blood was gushing out like a geyser. She was calm; he was cursing. "#%&*! I'm so stupid! How could this possibly happen!" he exclaimed. "Damn, ratzenfrass, argh, dangblasted thing!" I was confused and the woman scolded him and told him to quiet down. Blood continued to gush. I could only assume he had been shot, but now was no time to ask. He continued to curse loudly. We were the only ones in the room and

I really didn't know where I should look or what I should say. So I stared and said nothing.

Within a minute, the emergency room doctor and nurse came sprinting out of nowhere shouting, "What happened?" I started to explain my car had spun out of control on the highway when the doctor said, "Not you! Him!" The woman interrupted and explained that the man in the chair was her husband. She started to say, "My damn husband," when he interrupted her. "I cut my hand off with the table saw," which was followed by "Stupid!" He was suddenly calm, uncomfortably calm. He was talking as if he were mad about the Yankees losing. The doctor said, "Sir, you are in shock," to which the man retorted, "I'm not in no damn shock! I'm an idiot! I know better." My problems were diminishing before my very eyes. I began wondering why I was even there and I believe I may have called myself a wimp.

About this time, I noticed the automatic emergency room doors kept opening and closing for no apparent reason and each time, icy cold blasts of wind blew into the waiting room. Mayhem ensued. The nurse wheeled the man into an area right next to me and pulled the curtain closed while he continued stammering, "Jeez, damn, stupid, rutzenfrussen thing!" I kept wondering why I was there.

Soon, I overheard the nurse and the doctor whispering to each other. "Uh, do you know, I mean, did you ask, uh, where's the hand?" I couldn't believe what I was hearing. I became intrigued. If I had any physical injuries, they certainly took a back seat to this conversation. *Zip, clunk*, went the automatic doors again. And again, the icy blast. I turned to see who could be coming in to this sideshow. No one was there. I began to think the hospital was haunted. The nurse suggested, "Should we ask the wife?" Now I became nervous. The man was still swearing loudly at himself. The doctor offered painkillers and other drugs, but the man's response was, "I don't need no stinkin' drugs! I need my stupid hand!"

*Zip, clunk.* Again went the doors. Again, the winter wind. The nurse got brave enough to ask the wife about the hand and she said, "We brought it with us; it was on his lap." I almost vomited; now I had a reason to be in the emergency room. The nurse whispered to the doctor, "Uh, she said it's here somewhere." *Zip, clunk.* Just then, I looked at the floor where the automatic doors kept opening and realized the thing that was making the doors open and close was not a ghost. I pointed to the floor, gagging. "Thing" on the *Addams Family* was the closest I had ever been to this kind of thing, no pun intended.

The nurse and doctor retrieved the hand, put it in a bucket of ice, and called a helicopter to airlift the man to a neighboring trauma center. He was cursing the entire way. I thought to myself, as the maintenance staff mopped up the area, "There goes the toughest guy I've ever seen."

I simply rose and walked out of the room, looking for a phone to call a cab. As I left the area, the nurse, who had composed herself rather quickly I'll admit, called out to me, "Sir, the doctor will be with you in a few minutes." I smiled and shook my head. "That's okay. I'm good. Really. I'm good." *Zip, clunk.*

# Things everyone should try (again)...

- Play hangman with your spouse out on the deck

- Consume a root beer float, using only the straw

- Try to hula hoop for exactly twenty seconds, ten in each direction

- Bark at your dog and wait for a response

- Pop Rocks and a Pepsi

- Put a leaf on your hand while making an "O" and smack it to make it pop

- Silly String and make sure you get it in the hair

- Silly putty on the comics section of a newspaper

- Count to three, just like Count Chocula

- See how many apples you can hold in one hand; bananas in the other

- Sail a paper airplane out the second floor window

- Tiptoe through someone's tulips. If they demand your name, blame it on "Tim."

- Name your dog "Stay" for a day

- Backwards somersault

- Answer the phone "One ringy dingy" and see what they say

- Record yourself trying to get a baby to smile

- Look in your closet and compare the number of shoes you own to those you actually wear

- Reach into your couch cushions and play "name that item" before pulling it out

- Find an old episode of the Carol Burnet show and watch Mr. Tudball and Mrs. Wiggins

- Put on someone else's glasses when they are not looking

- Find out exactly how many licks it takes to get to the center of a Tootsie Roll Pop

- Mow the lawn, but do your initials

- Move your refrigerator out and find out what was behind and under it

- Hold a cat upside down and watch her flip to her feet; then try it with your spouse

- Ask the cashier at the dollar store if there's a clearance rack

# Halloween

Halloween is my least favorite "holiday," and I'm not even sure it is one. I never really got it as a kid. I went around, usually as a sheet with two eyeholes, and brought home a pillowcase of candy. Sometimes we would go to a house and they would give us a toothbrush or a banana. I can only assume the toothbrush was from a dentist's personal residence and the latter was from a produce manager, but who knows. It always seemed like it was snowing on Halloween night, too. I remember when I finally found a decent costume, my mom would make me wear a parka over it because I would "catch my death of cold," whatever that meant. A ghost wearing a parka wasn't scaring anyone. I think they gave me treats because they felt sorry for me. "Here little boy; I mean....oooh, scary goblin from Alaska. Have a toothbrush."

When I was a kid, you could go trick or treating without Mom and Dad following you around in a car. And it was dark. We would go up on porches, ring the bell, and holler "trick or treat?" The grumpy dad would sometimes say, "Don't you kids get enough candy in your lives that you need a whole bag in one day?" The old, crotchety grandfather who looked like he had just chopped up neighbors in the woodshed behind the house would say, "Git the hell outa my yard; I know where you live!" We had no idea who he was and he didn't have a clue who our parents were, but we ran anyway. Most often, we'd get a nice mom who would drop five or six Twix or Three Musketeers bars in our bags and we would be happy.

I would get home and dad always needed to "inspect" the merchandise, reminding us that there are crazy people out there who put razor blades in candy. Of course he would sample each and every piece to say that he was testing them. I would eat just about everything left in the bag. I remember having to go to the dentist one time, and our family doctor rhetorically asked me, "You've been eating a lot of junk, haven't you?" I didn't respond. He followed with, "I give out toothbrushes at Halloween for kids like you!" I knew it.

# Saturday Saling

As the President of the Chamber of Commerce and one looking to enhance the quality of life in our community and business environment, instead of turning to Forbes, Fortune, Harvard Business School, and other academics for marketing concepts, best practices, and selling strategies, one only needs to look at the indispensible, irrefutable, incomprehensible phenomena of Garage "Saling." You see, my mother and her friends trek weekly across lands far and wide, with GPS in hand, and newspaper classifieds in their clutch, to scope the path for a day's journey to the never-ending list of garage, yard, estate, lawn, multi-family, and porch sales.

The key to their success is to first prepare their game plan, just as a head football coach would draw up plays for the coming Sunday showdown. MARKER...check. NEWSPAPER...check. GPS...check. GEOGRAPHIC ORDER OF SALES...check. DRIVER...check. SCOUTS...check. PLENTY OF ONE DOLLAR BILLS...check. COFFEE...check. Then, the "mission" begins.

The goal is to score a touchdown, of course. In garage sale terms, this would mean finding something that someone wants to sell for a quarter and getting them talked down to a nickel. Very seldom is the item a necessity; in fact, the sale's importance overtakes the item's worth. The thrill of the hunt is greater than the sum of its parts. The process is greater than the result. The form is greater than the function. The collective bargaining that takes place on a weekly basis is more involved than the NFL Players Association and Owners agreements. My mother can walk into a garage sale with $1.00, come out with three shirts, a purse, a moss-covered three-handled family credenza and $.75 in her pocket. Her friends will say, "They wanted that much? Couldn't you talk them down? That credenza is used. Take it back." She will bring her treasure back to my loving father, who will ask her, "What are we going to do with three kids' shirts?" Mom will reply, "They're new and still in the package," not really providing the answer he was looking for.

The team consists of my mother and her two friends. Occasionally, a "sub" who has mastered the art of "saling" is included. If you are new to the team, by privilege you get to ride in the back. You are not allowed to talk. Your job is to provide support only. You are able to add some occasional comments such as, "That purse is beautiful," but you are not allowed to question the sale, the price, or the quality of the product. However, if you are a veteran, you have a meaningful job. You may be asked to drive, survey the territory, inspect, and provide referrals, like a color commentator on ESPN. This status comes with knowledge, experience, and practice of the secret handshake, which they have not yet shared with me.

The husbands' roles are to, of course, poke fun at the team while having coffee, golfing, fishing, or eating breakfast. Most likely they are wearing the shirts found at garage sales, drinking from cups found at yard sales, and eating with good old Oneida silverware, found at estate sales. The silverware is a "touchdown" as it once sold for $29.99, but was recently purchased by a team member for 25 cents. It is the husbands' privilege to eat from a "touchdown."

There is very little advertising involved, no billboards, radio spots, television commercials, or planes flying with banners. The entire market takes place underground. Training is free. Certification is not necessary. There are no quality control mechanisms, SWOT analyses, strategic planning indexes, or identity profiles. The entire process happens by word of mouth. It may just be that "saling" is the best and most efficient form of marketing there is. One only needs to sit in a lawn chair and watch the passersby and their bargaining skills to see the magnificent wonder of the Art of Selling at work. Of course, the chair you are sitting in can be sold too, if there is a taker and if the price is right.

# Dignity and Determination

Each day, I have the wonderful opportunity to watch seniors at the YMCA using the Wellness Center and pool. It is amazing to see those with walkers, canes, and wheelchairs make it up the sidewalk, slowly and deliberately, during winter snowstorms and hot summer days. As they enter the building, I can't help but think of the courage and strength it must take to first, get up and get going in the morning; second, get ready for exercising; and third, work out hard. It's difficult to do that even at my age.

Not only are these troupers strong physically, they display emotional courage, too. Even after losing a spouse, family member, or friend, they continue their regime, disciplined and strong. The rest of the people in their water classes or on treadmills next to them become family and support systems. It is not uncommon to see people at the Y with prosthetic arms or legs walking next to someone who is hearing or visually impaired. Each day, these friends look forward to catching up with each other, genuinely concerned about the others' lives, struggles, and successes. When I think of these folks, it always humbles me. Whatever aches and pains I may have quickly subside.

A couple of years ago, a wonderful 93-year old gentleman came to the Y three days a week. He had Post-Polio Syndrome. Although he struggled to walk, when he got in the pool, he became like a child again - walking, even running, in place. Don was an amazing man. I came to know him personally and he invited me to his home just before he passed away. He had told me in advance that he was an entertainer for the USO back in

World War II. He had been a magician and had traveled the world. It wasn't until I stepped into his basement and saw photos of him with Laurel and Hardy, Abbott and Costello, Marilyn Monroe, Jack Benny, and others, that I learned his story.

Don would drive himself to the Y each time and walk the long and difficult trek up the sidewalk. He would come to the desk to present his membership card, but with both hands turned over and closed into fists. He would ask you to pick a hand. No matter which hand you chose, it would ultimately result in five or six red balls and the membership card in the one you didn't. Not long after he passed, we created an award in his honor to recognize people who overcome physical challenges to achieve their goals. He was, and continues to be, an inspiration to me and hundreds of others for his determination.

I typically hear, "It's tough to get old," from many of our seniors. They share their challenges and I know that someday I will have mine, as well. To me, they are teachers, showing me how to grow older with dignity, strength, and humor. I will remember and reflect on my friend Don as time passes, and try my best to maintain a great spirit, encouraging others to do the same.

# Another Day That Will Live in Infamy

Sometimes I ask people where they were on 9/11 just to hear how the news of that tragic day in our history affected them. There are so many stories and answers and experiences, all different, that people share. In my case, I remember I was holding our regularly scheduled Tuesday morning YMCA management team meeting. The wellness center staff person interrupted our meeting (which very seldom happens) and said, "You might want to come and see this." We all walked into the wellness center where normally the televisions are showing ESPN or the Travel Channel. We stood, watching replays of the first plane hitting the Tower. I remember all of us commenting, "Why would a plane be flying so low?" We thought the pilot must have had difficulty and accidentally hit the building. We looked at the clock and said, "Oh my God, it's after 8:00AM; people are probably working in there." And then there was silence.

When the second plane hit the second tower, it was clear to us that this was no accident. In fact, we were all a little scared. There were news reports flashing all over the place that more planes had been hijacked and the "attack" was coming in various forms in Washington, Atlanta, Boston, and other big cities. In Rome, New York, we knew Griffiss was a contractor for the military and probably a strategic site. It seemed like the world was under attack. We didn't know by whom, but we feared we might be a possible target. The President looked disheveled. The fear grew worse. Then we heard jets were being scrambled out of Rome. It was such a surreal few moments, like a movie. We drive in and around Griffiss, now a business park, nearly every day. To hear jets are being scrambled really created a sense of panic.

This was followed quickly by sadness, as our collective jaws were on the floor, watching all of those people scurrying for safety among the rubble and ruins. I remember becoming angry - I mean really angry. "Who could do this to us? Why do they hate us so much that they would kill innocent people? What did we do to them? Why is this happening?" I remember wanting revenge.

Looking back on that day now, I think about how much our lives have changed. I think about the vacation I took last week, and all of the precautionary measures now in place that weren't in place then. I think about all of the memorials, dedications, speeches, benefit concerts, sacrifices, military efforts, loss of families, survivors, war, and turmoil. I think about the human stories that emerged, the stories of rescue, the pulling together of a nation and the renewed significance of the American flag. I realize now that the happy little world I thought we lived in is not so rosy and life isn't that easy. It's complicated.

Although I have always looked at life through positive eyes and tried to find the best in people, that day made me realize not everyone feels the same way. The hatred runs long and deep. There are people in other countries who don't even know me, but who literally hate me, what my freedom stands for, and my way of living. Over time, that anger I had turned into courage and appreciation for what I have.

Now, I have this little thing I do. Every time I happen to look at my watch or the clock and, just by chance, it reads "9:11," I say a little prayer for the families who lost loved ones that day. I also thank God for those that served as heroes. No one who woke up that morning had any idea of what that day would bring. But we got through it and it has made us who we are, stronger, wiser, and hopefully more appreciative.

# Books and Beaches

I decided on Sunday to do two of my favorite things: sit on the floor at Barnes & Noble and read, and take my dog for a walk at Verona Beach. Barnes & Noble is great because I get to grab a new book, order coffee, and read on the floor. Where else, other than home, can you find such comfort? I think I could live there. There are way too many choices of coffee, however. The latte, double latte, macchiato, espresso, double espresso, frappuchino, cappuccino…good Lord. I decided on the Casino Racino Ricardo Montalbano Vinnie Barbarino. I can't read it all; there's a lot of banging and clanging when they make it, and I think hot milk is involved, so I just tell them "Number Two," not even knowing what it is. Warm milk makes me sleepy anyway, as does reading, and it would be embarrassing to fall asleep on the floor at a bookstore. The teenaged attendant appeared miraculously from a cloud of steam, offering me a cup with my name on it.

I chose three books: *The Story*, which is the story of the Bible in chronological order; Steve Martin's *Pure Drivel*; and Mark Twain's *Roughing It*. Do you think maybe I could find three more different books? It was very busy there. Apparently Bill Cosby was in the store signing his new book; at first, I thought it was the line for the coffee. Seeing this gave me the idea to write my own book. I think I'll call it "Random Ramblings about Those Who Read Them" or something like that. I can't imagine anyone waiting in line to have me sign anything. Plus, he's Bill Cosby for God's sake! I'd better have good coffee. I took my books and left for the beach.

The walk in Verona Beach was awesome. It was such a windy day that the seagulls were only able to hover. They looked like kites. As my dog did his best to jump up and catch the seagulls, I walked around the shore and thought about how tough things can be on the holidays for people who are struggling. I'm not sure why that thought just popped in my head while I was sitting there, but it did. I think it was because I saw others sitting alone on park benches or going for a walk with their dogs. I realized that maybe I'm lonely too. I sat down on the rocks and wrote this as I looked up in the sky:

In a cloud I can see a trace of sunshine
In a storm I can see a lighthouse
The lights are rays of hope that seek you
Don't be afraid to notice them
And you won't feel so alone

I came home and wrote this for my weekly column. Even though I might be feeling a little lonely, I don't feel so alone. A bunch of other people were doing the same thing today. A book and a nap might be exactly what I need. Tomorrow will be a better day.

# My Top Ten Ideas to Improve the World

1. Bring back *Schoolhouse Rock* to teach politics and English. It's how I learned how a bill becomes a law. It's how I learned what an adverb is.
2. Have everyone's cell phone numbers be their license plate numbers. If you don't like their driving, call them up. Tell them.
3. Replace all guns with feathers. If you really want to kill someone, it has to be through tickle torture.
4. GPS for socks. 'Nuff said.
5. Glasses with autofocus lenses. We'd only have to purchase one pair of glasses for our entire life. Like a camera, you just adjust to the distance as you get older.
6. A washing machine that also dries. Just add another cycle. Once the spin cycle is over, the next section is heat and drying.
7. Celebrate special days nationally. Create "No Texting Tuesdays." If you want to send someone a message, you actually have to pick up the phone and speak with them. "No Whining Wednesdays." Every complaint has to be replaced with a compliment. "Free Fridays." Gas is free every Friday. So is pizza. The President has to declare it, and we all have to abide by it.
8. A phone app that gets rid of everyone's phone apps

9. Add two more hours to a day. There should be nothing wrong with 26. We could all use a couple of extra hours. Although saying, "Man, I'm working 26/7" doesn't sound very good.

10. All of the celebrities who have one name have to try to make it on talent alone. At risk are: Madonna, Cher, Ciara, Brandy, Avant, Seal, Sinbad, Yanni and Shakira.

# Does This Only Happen to Me?

Ah, life's little challenges. I am not sure if I'm the only one out there who has these things happen to them, but these happen to me all the time.

I just bought new wiper blades and they clean everything except my line of sight for traffic. I sometimes circle the parking lot at Wal-Mart three or four times trying to find a close spot instead of parking right where I am and walking the extra ten feet. My bag of Tostitos Scoops is half air. I will wait until my shoelace completely breaks before getting a new one, and complain about the lace instead of my procrastination. When I snowblow the driveway, inevitably the snow blows back in my face regardless of the direction I'm walking. I could make a bed out of used dryer sheets. When it's really sunny out, it simply sheds light on how dusty my house is, even after I clean it (where does the dust come from anyway?). I never really know when I need a new toothbrush. I think when it spreads out like wings; it's time for a new one. I own a hairbrush and I am not sure why. I can never find a rubber band when I need one, but paper clips are everywhere. I really do not know why an opened box of Arm & Hammer Baking Soda helps my refrigerator, but I've always had one in there. The other day I exclaimed that "my vacuum cleaner sucks" and realized I was giving it a compliment. I recognized that when I buy coffee and bottled water every day, if I added it up for the year, that could be two extra mortgage payments. I don't understand why ironing boards are narrow on one end. I'm not sure what razors are made of, but again, that's another mortgage payment; maybe it's a bad thing that a sharp blade is battery-operated and vibrates. I'm pretty sure I only need one pair of tweezers for my whole lifetime, but I have several.

I dropped my lint brush on the floor the other day, after I had vacuumed, and it was covered with dog hair, confirming my vacuum's disability. I thought of inventing a six-foot lint brush to use on carpets. I never throw away t-shirts because I reason that they all bring back a memory. I have a treadmill that serves as a part-time laundry basket. I have hundreds of books, but have never read any of them more than once. I have bars of soap that I think are pretty old, but I won't throw them away because I'm not sure if soap gets dirty or outdated. I sold a shirt in my mom's garage sale. I think she found it at another one a year later and bought it for me as a gift, saying, "I thought you'd like this one. It looks like something you might wear." Lastly, I had to stop on my road the other day to watch a squirrel dart back and forth making up his mind as to which side was safer; I get confused like that too.

To all of the little things that make us smile - thank you!

# Captain's Log

On a beautiful Sunday morning, my friend John asked me and my friend Pauline to go out on his boat. He is new to the boating hobby and bought a twenty-two foot cabin cruiser. Most people start with a canoe. Other friends and family were invited to go, but they had other things to do that day, so it was just the three of us.

After about fifteen minutes, heading into the canal, near the mouth of the lake, we slowed down to admire the pristine water, and hundreds of other boat enthusiasts getting ready for a great day. I threw out a fishing line, and had trolled for a few moments, when the boat came to an abrupt stop in the middle of the canal. "What was that, John?" I asked. Captain John responded, "I don't know; I think we might have hit something." No water was coming into the boat, but it was clear we were on top of something big because when we put the motor in the water and went forward, it stood still. When we hit reverse, the same happened. Mind you, there were hundreds on the pier gazing out at us, and dozens of boats passing by. I could see people snickering. "Need a hand?" was a common comment. "No, we're fine, just stuck on something," was our reply.

We were only about a hundred feet from shore, and the canal was very shallow. Swimming to the shore would have been no problem, but we didn't want to get wallets, purses, or cell phones wet, so we waited. And, we waited. A passerby came up and said, "Need a tow?" We said, "Sure. See what you can do." We threw him the rope and he tied it to his boat and pulled, but our boat only spun in circles, gaining no relief from the mysterious underwater hazard we were on. We asked if the man and his friend could summon the authorities when they got to shore and they said they would. I continued fishing and eating peanuts.

About an hour later, the authorities pulled up to our boat and asked if they could tow us. We had random, sarcastic thoughts, but said, "Yep. Good idea." After fifteen minutes of trying, it was clear that the boat wasn't going anywhere. There was a lot of scraping noises, and we didn't think that sounded good. They said they wanted to go in and get a bigger boat, but as they started to leave, the stern began to fill up quickly with water. We asked to climb aboard and they said to jump in, helping all three of us to safety. We went to shore and filled out reports and talked to people. Several asked us as we were walking if we had heard about a boat sinking. We looked out to our former spot, and could see the vessel beginning to capsize. It was going down. We went into a restaurant and ordered lunch, while the boat gradually sank to its watery grave.

We didn't think too much of it at all; after all, we hadn't been in much danger. It was actually a little humorous, especially because the official name of the boat was "Rescue Me." We arranged for a ride home from friends and proceeded to hear several news accounts about three people being rescued from a sinking boat on Oneida Lake. It was everywhere. John was interviewed by every radio, television, and newspaper in the area. There had been a serious accident just days before, so the media was linking our story to the safety of boating on the lake, and we were victims of bad timing. Luckily, our incident was an inconvenience, not a matter of life and death.

The next day, I went back to work and wrote my weekly column as readers wanted to know what had happened to us. We took a lot of ribbing for our adventure and I thought it would be okay to write about our "final moments" at sea, but not make light of the dangers of boating. The rescue squad from the county and village did an awesome job and we were very thankful for their help. Here is my column, verbatim:

This is the last entry from the log of Captain John Ready's cruiser "Rescue Me."

Captain's Log, Star Date 7-9-12:

12:05PM: "I am aboard the vessel appropriately named 'Rescue Me' just off the shore of Oneida Lake. The winds are strong, as is the will of the crew."

12:11PM: First-Mate: "Captain John, I believe we have struck an iceberg."

Captain: "Check that, seaman. I'll have a look-see. We are in shallow waters; depth-finder reports 12 feet. I'll stay with the boat. Send the girl overboard to investigate."

12:12PM: Girl: "Why Me?"

12:13 PM: First-Mate: "Sir, I believe we are balancing on something. I see no water in the vessel. It appears we are fine. Our food supplies are low, though, as we are out of peanuts."

*Don't Rock the Boat* by the Hues Corporation is playing on the stereo.

12:14 PM: Small canoe passes by; sounds of chuckling can be heard from a distance.

12:15 PM: First-Mate: "Excuse me…Sir, (to the canoe captain) permission to board?"

Canoe Operator: "No."

12:16 PM: Girl: "Captain, there is a small pool forming in the bow. A bag of Jax is submerged."

Captain John: "I'll take those."

12:17 PM: First-Mate: "Captain, I think I have a fish on line. Are we going to be stuck long?"

Captain John: "I'm working on it."

12:18 PM: Girl: "Captain, I don't mean to be a pain, but my feet are getting wet."

Captain John: "Suck it up, buttercup. I'll hit the bilge pump."

Captain's Log, Star Date 7-9-12:

12:20 PM: "Rescue Me" apparently has rested on an unknown, underwater object, balancing perfectly on the hull. My crew seems to be planning a mutiny. My crew is safe. I am safe. Maybe I should abort this whole "Captain goes down with the boat" concept and let them fend for themselves. No, wait. I can't do that. They'll never go with me again. Stick it out just a few more moments. Just a few more.

12:21PM: Captain John: "First-Mate Leo, what are you taking pictures of?"

First Mate: "Your insurance claim, sir."

12:22PM: Arrival of passerby in small rowboat.

12:23 PM: "You guys need a tow?"

Captain John: "Mayday, mayday."

First-Mate and Girl to Captain: "Captain, wait for us!"

12:25 PM: Authorities arrive. "Hop in folks; we'll take you to safety. You must be stuck on something big. Our boat can't even tow it."

12:30 PM: Captain (after two hours): "I'll have the beef on a wreck, please."

# Sunday Mornings

Ever since I can remember, Sunday mornings have been very special to me. My fondest memory as a kid was that of waking up early with my PJs on, and sitting on the floor in the living room. While my mom made "pizza frit" (no, not fried dough), Dad would join me and we'd watch Abbott & Costello movies. I remember our favorite being "Abbott & Costello Meet Frankenstein." It had Wolfman, Dracula, and all of the scary monsters of the day, but it was hilarious. It was always followed by *F Troop*. Then, as soon as the movie was over…outside! Baseball, basketball, football, a walk, a bike ride, you name it - but no video games, that's for sure. If it was winter, we shoveled off the court and played anyway. If it was summer, we didn't come home until the streetlights came on. Later in the day, it was time for supper (not dinner). Supper was always macaroni (not pasta) and it was with the whole family. Dad helped in the kitchen with cooking by sampling each pot; mom threw him out. My sisters threw their peas down the register to avoid eating them, and I tried to retrieve them because peas are my favorite.

Now, Sundays are still my favorite day of the week. Sometimes it's yard work or mowing the lawn. Sometimes it's cleaning the house. I still go outside, walk the dog, go for a bike ride, or just lounge around. But every time, it ends with a movie and supper. I never go out to eat on a Sunday. There's just something about being home and enjoying your time. Whether it's going to church, having friends over for a cookout (not grilling), playing catch in the yard, or a painting project - Sundays are special days.

Every once in a while, I pop in my Abbott & Costello DVD and watch one of the old movies while enjoying some chili made on the stove, or better yet some of Dad's chili that he made on his stove and dropped off. It always brings me back to a wonderful peace and calm that, despite the hectic days of our lives, should never end.

# A Boxful of Memories

Over the weekend, I was going through my basement to clear out some "debris." I came upon an old box and opened it, only to find a smattering of school notes, books, and a collection of grade reports I thought I would share. It was buried under a small stack of 45s which included: "Little Willy" from The Sweet; "Bad Blood" from Neil Sedaka; "Heartbeat, It's a Love Beat," from the DeFranco Family; "Saturday Night" from the Bay City Rollers; and "Sometimes When We Touch" from Dan Hill…pure sap. Must have been my sister's box, is all I can think. I'm not sure who wrote "Hank's…Don't touch!" on it.

Underneath was a treasure trove of papers in a makeshift scrapbook. I would first like to call attention to the fact that Sister Mary Alberto, a teacher at Saint Joseph's School of Religion, stated, "Henry is a very fine boy." Apparently I wasn't all that fine to Sister, because the next paper underneath was a form with checkmarks on: Being Dependable, Being Cheerful, Sharing, Listening When Others Speak, and Trying Hard to Learn. "Paying Attention" was not checked. Hmm. Next paper: "Playground Award - Oneida Youth Bureau/Allen Park." No, I did not get 1st Place in the Kickball Tournament. Instead, I snared a whopping 4th Place Award in the Talent Show. It's hard to conceive there were three others who could balance brooms on their noses, but it more than likely was a political decision. Scott "Mr. Everything" probably took first. He took first in everything and deservedly so. On to the Pinewood Derby Award from Cub Scouts, on May 12, 1973. I captured 3rd Place in "The Derby." I don't even recall there being three in the competition. I only remember my friend Donny. So, I am pretty sure I could lobby to have it corrected to 2nd Place if I wanted to. The next sheet, folded into a football, was a pencil-drawn stick figure wearing a baseball cap. I assume this was a self-portrait that was created during lunch, where we flicked it through finger-made field goalposts.

Next is Mr. Midlam's critique of my amazing Math progress. "Still convinced Hank should be doing straight E work," writes Rit. I am hoping E is considered excellent, however there is no key. Apparently, I was having trouble with decimals. This was followed by Mr. Fragola's 1976 Junior High report, where I was rumored to have been disturbing the peace in Room 302. "Hank needs to stop talking to the kids next to him," notes Mr. F. On to 1979, where Mr. Corona awarded me a stellar 81 in Math Course I. I will not hold this against him, however his YMCA membership dues just went up. The next page is an Oneida Indians 1980 Football Roster, where I am listed at 5'7" (generously) and 141 pounds (I wish). Looking at these weights, I don't know how we did it. Our offensive line was Shawn Ryan (153); Ed Barker (159), Gary Whipple (171), and Fred Widger (166).

The next page is an ACT Score and recommendation that I study "Journalism;" go figure. Lastly, there is a letter from Athletic Director Bill Farriel (Yes, I received the Bill Farriel Award. Thank you, Rotary. I am humbled and very honored.) informing parents of our baseball team's trip to Leominster, MA, next to a photo of our crazy team. I remember getting our collective tails whipped, but we had a great trip.

The last sheet in the box is a drawing by Yours Truly of who I think is either Mr. Carruthers from Junior High, or Uncle Fester from the Addams Family; I cannot be sure.

I don't know why I kept this box of memories. Most people keep things from their childhood that they are proud of, like maybe a first-place ribbon, or an "A" report card. Not me. I think life ends up being one big box of collective stuff that you learn from. Ironically, in my career now, I work with the Cub Scouts and host the Pinewood Derby at the YMCA once a year. I still talk a lot during seminars to the people I'm with. Unfortunately, I am still 5'7". I draw cartoons once in a while when I'm bored, and I've written a book. Sister Mary Alberto would be proud.

# The Greatest Time of the Year

As we enjoy some wonderful Central New York weather, almost spring-like in recent weeks, and head toward the holidays, I cannot help but think of what our world has become. I hear frequently that Christmas is now just a moneymaking gimmick for retailers and big companies to push product. Maybe it's that Christmas carols start playing on the radio now before Thanksgiving. It just doesn't feel right to hear "Chestnuts roasting on an open fire" when it's still 80 degrees out.

We talk about "Black Friday" and "Cyber Monday" almost as if they are holidays themselves. Every year we hear of people trampled at a discount store fighting for a place in line, hunters being shot and killed accidentally during the first few days of deer season, child abuse, and exploitation. On one side of the coin, the world looks like a terrible place. I would like to offer that although the incidents are real and it may seem that the moral fiber of our community is deteriorating, there is still enough good in the world, plenty of hope, and an overwhelming amount of caring, joy, and peace among us to be thankful and appreciative.

If you let the bad take over, it will. If you let crime, anarchy, and disregard take precedence, it will. If you let despair and hatred rule, it will. The reverse is also true. Look around you for a moment. Watch the volunteers on a cold winter night ring the bell for the Salvation Army for the poor and needy. Listen to the lyrics of a traditional Christmas song and appreciate the message that gets so easily clouded. Watch children being born, those with cancer fighting for their lives and showing strength and determination, those without jobs continuing to search, and those who protect children never giving up in making our schools, businesses, and homes safer. Just because times get tough, or challenges get steep, there is no reason to quit. There is way too much at stake and giving up should never be an option. The definition of hope and faith is believing that good can and will prevail, regardless of the size of the mountain, the numbers against you, or the cards stacked in the deck. In many people's cases, hope is all they have. Let's not let it get lost in the shuffle.

If we cut back this year on presents, let us not cut back on giving of ourselves. In times like these, people need help more than ever. Surround those in need with plenty of love and support, a little at a time, becoming progressively more and more generous. To those who question "Why?" may your response, corny or not, be "Why not?"

# Christmas at the Leo Home

Christmas always brings back great memories. I vividly remember sitting upstairs on my bed, excited to run downstairs and open presents. I remember it always being cold outside, with plenty of snow - the kind that glistens in the moonlight and streetlamps when you look out the window. Every once in a while, I would hear a distant noise. My transistor radio would track Santa coming our way from faraway lands. The radio stations would always let us know when the Big Guy was getting closer to our area. Unfortunately now, we have Storm Tracker and Accuweather Forecasts to tell us when we are getting blizzards. They should do the same to track Santa. I am sure he has a GPS and listens to the Garmin Lady about how to get to Oneida. He might get as confused as we do now. "Turn left," "Turn left," "Turn left," and Santa's sleigh is going in a circle. "Recalculating…"

Once I heard the noise, I would look outside to see if he was there. There would be noises all over the house. I would sneak down the stairs only to find half-eaten chocolate chip cookies and a half glass of milk. I would sit on the register to stay warm and wait until it was okay to "be awake." I would ask Mom and Dad "Is it time yet?" and Dad would always respond, "It's four in the morning, go back to bed!" Of course, now that he was awake, it was time. My sister Terri would wake everyone else up and we would sit under the tree and start ripping open presents. Mom would grab the camera and start snapping pictures; Dad would get a big garbage bag and start stuffing it with the wrappings. There would be fried dough cooking on the stove, with a mound of sugar for rolling.

The Yule Log was on television and the classic carols were softly playing in the background. Even though at the time, opening up a new whiffle ball set, or a toy truck, or a family game, was awesome, just the scene of sitting together with our family, all in the same room sharing love and joy, was enough to make the day worth living. I was always as excited to give presents as I was to receive them. I loved seeing their faces when paper and ribbons were flying everywhere.

Merry Christmas to everyone. May the joy and spirit of this season bring you hope and comfort. Looking back over my childhood, it was the memories of being together that made holidays, and every day, special. I wish that for everyone.

# Some Statistics

Percentage of people who drive slowly in front of me when I am in a hurry: 100

Number of times this year the copier at work has a paper jam when I use it: 5,324; everyone else combined: 5

Number of times I've been solicited to get a new credit card this month: 30

Number of people who bought a membership to the YMCA on January 2nd: 136; number still working out on February 2nd: 3

Number of times today I wrote "LOL": 14; actual times I laughed out loud: 0

Percentage of kids at the Y who ask me where my hair went: 87

Number of miles over on my oil change sticker: 11,469

Number of channels I have on Time Warner: 1019; number viewed: 3

Amount of topics I think of in line at the DMV: 256

Average number of magazines I thumb through at the doctor's office waiting room: 26; number of those magazines I would purchase: 0

Number of glaucoma air puff tests I have had in five years: 5; number of times in my life I have had whiplash: 5

Average height of a Leo family member: 5'0"; what it would be if I weren't here: 4'2"

Number of times throughout the baseball season I heard Coach Frank DiChristina yell, "Go Yankees!": 162; number of times I have heard anyone yell, "Go Mets!": 1 (Me)

World's record for the length of a general staring contest: 32.2 hours; average length of a staring contest between me and the little kid at the Y: 3.4 seconds (I always break first)

Amount of time I can balance a broom on my nose: 43 seconds; percentage of times the broom hits me in the forehead: 96

Percentage of times I have washed my car just before a heavy rain: 93

Percentage of times I have snowblown the driveway in the morning and it has melted in the afternoon: 98

# iCan't Connect

Over the weekend, I thought it would be a good project to rearrange my stereo, computer, television, and sound system. I am an Apple guy, so I have an iMac, an iPhone, an iPod, and iPad and I wanted to connect them all together. I asked some professional questions online, did some research, and came up with the solution to get Apple TV. No, it is not a mini-television; instead it links all of your "stuff." As I began connecting things and running wires all over the house, it became clear I didn't know what I was doing. I plugged in everything according to the manuals, coordinated all of the equipment, drew a diagram, plugged everything in, and no sound. On my hands and knees, sprawling on the floor and pressing hundreds of buttons on my receiver, the only sound I could produce was two grunts and a groan. "Aha! I exclaimed." The only thing not on was the "On" button on the receiver. To hear Bon Jovi's "Livin' On a Prayer" in ear-piercing, off-the-charts decibels in my right ear with my face right next to the speaker is an experience I wouldn't wish on anyone. For the rest of the day, my balance was off, I kept leaning to the left, and I was humming background harmonies to that now-awful song.

The good news is that I can now play a song from my bathroom on my playlist, on my television from the bedroom, watch slideshows, movies, and videos in the basement, and synch music from my phone to the computer and iPod while in the closet. Confused? Me too. Last night, when a call came in, I think I answered the toaster. It would not surprise me if my new waffle iron can now show Lady Gaga music videos. Once everything is connected, it is pretty amazing. I watched a YouTube video on my phone in the bathroom, while the Rebirth Brass Band was cranked in the kitchen. Excessive stimuli. It would be like if you went to your local movie theatre and all of the individual movie doors were open and you were in the hallway.

I started to dig out a space for my new vegetable garden (I will discuss this another time), and was listening to music coming from the spare room. I thought it would be cool to have music outside as well, and looked online and saw that they make speakers now that look like rocks. You put the speaker in the garden and music comes from the dirt. I keep thinking this might just be a bad idea altogether. I can see myself throwing the rock into the woods (because I'm trying to get rid of rocks), then I would hear Bon Jovi coming from the cliff in my back yard. If anyone needs help mounting speakers, synching technology, creating a listening experience, please call a professional. I'll be in the garden.

# Life Lessons from Charlie Brown

A number of years ago, I worked in a variety of youth programs. I spent a lot of time with some really tough kids who were at risk of dropping out of school, didn't have many friends, lacked in social skills, and felt like they didn't fit in. They were at risk of alcohol and substance abuse, teen pregnancy, truancy, and in some cases, worse. I volunteered my time at one point in five different youth organizations simultaneously because I love kids, know how important they are to our future, and felt that I could help play a part in making them feel worthwhile. Each day was a new challenge and the problems I learned about were like mountains to these kids and they did not know how to overcome them. I thought that buried inside every at-risk kid is a soul that is dying to succeed. I always believed that by listening to them, getting to know where they were coming from and how they felt helped me to understand where to start in working with them on their path. I guess I truly believed that if you reached in, got all the goop off them, and found the true kid underneath, he or she was just waiting to shine. Many years removed from being a youth leader, these feelings are something I have taken with me as an employer, a friend, and hopefully, a brother.

As I was thumbing through a box of papers from those days recently, I came across a letter. I remember writing to one of our country's greatest icons during a difficult period with the kids and asking for advice on how to help them. It seems so funny now that I would write a letter to Mr. Charles M. Schulz, creator of "Peanuts" about this sort of thing, but I did. Reading it, it seems to me just as important and appropriate now as it did then. He responded:

*Dear Mr. Leo:*

*While it would, indeed, be wonderful if we lived in a world where there was no pain, sorrow, or injustice, it would be unrealistic to hope for considering the complex world in which we live.*

*Though everyone we encounter throughout our lives will not always be kind, honest, and fair, we can, even in the face of disappointment, use Charlie Brown as an example- refuse to give up and keep right on trying!*

*If someone should be unkind or rude to you, rather than react in like manner, it would be better to respond with a pleasantry or a kind gesture. In other words, never let someone else dictate your personality.*

*Best wishes to each of you as you pursue your goals, which in this country, are virtually unlimited.*

*Kindest regards,*

*Charles M. Schulz*

The letter is dated October 4, 1994. As you may know, Mr. Schulz passed away on February 12, 2000, only six years after writing this to me. Sometimes we get so far away from our core values and accept things as "it is what it is." But when I think about Mr. Schulz's kind words, it all boils down to the same thing - we need to treat people better. In our community, treating each other with kindness and respect should be "it is what it is." The next time you feel the need to get angry, frustrated, or discouraged, think of Charlie Brown. We could use more of him.

# Little League, with a Few Sprinkles

I have been removed from playing, coaching, and watching Little League baseball games for decades, but happened to drive by a game the other day in Syracuse and stopped to watch. When I was a young kid, baseball was everything to me. My hero was Hank Aaron. I wanted to stand like him, bat like him, run and throw like him. The fact that he was black, during an era when he was receiving death threats for breaking Babe Ruth's record, never caused me to think twice about loving him. I was more proud my name was the same as his. I played Little League baseball for Oneida Castle. My dad, like so many other dads then and now, was the coach, along with Jim Cavanagh and Tom Roberts.

I was a pitcher and outfielder. I think there was only one other pitcher than me and I pitched every other game. I can still remember to this day how nervous I was to pitch to guys like Fred Widger, who would hit everything I threw over that barbed-wired fence where Holy Cross Academy now sits. I would look over to my dad and to Mr. Cavanagh and get that smile and nod, no matter how badly I was throwing. My dad would come out and say, "Take a deep breath, Hank, and just throw to the glove like we do in the yard." Mr. Cavanagh would say, "Just have fun, Hank; it's baseball."

The majority of my practice did, in fact, come from the front yard. Every night after supper, Dad would grab our gloves and a ball. He'd roll me 50-100 grounders and tell me to "Get in front of it." Then he'd let me pitch to him. In my mind, I would pretend guys like Reggie Jackson or Pete Rose were up and I would try to strike them out. I didn't throw very hard, but my dad was great at getting me to throw to the mitt. Honestly, I was just happy to play catch. I could do that every day, all day.

The ball was from a bucket of dirty, brown balls and our mitts were so worked you could fold them and put them in your pocket.

When Dad was at work, my friends and I would go to the park and play by ourselves. Finding 17 other kids to play was easy. Adults weren't needed; we just organized ourselves. If a kid got upset or hurt, or something happened to the bat or the ball, we just figured it out. If a kid got mad and took the only ball we had home with him, we'd typically say, "Fine. Go home, baby, but leave your ball, please." Those were our practices.

During games, the umps were whoever would volunteer to help. The moms would sit on the grass and cheer, even if you struck out. Every kid played, even if you weren't that good. I don't ever remember any of our team getting mad about a kid making an error or becoming angry about who played and who didn't. We all wanted to play and we all made errors. Sure, we were disappointed when we lost or when we made mistakes, but when we got ice cream cones after the game, no one really cared much about whether we'd won or lost. Statistics weren't kept on individual kids. Usually a mom would keep score, and it would be in her particular method of doing so. An official hit was recorded as any time a kid hit the ball, whether anyone hit it or not. Maybe that's why we all thought we hit .750 or so. It didn't really matter. If we lost a game, you saw the kids you played against the next day anyway. "Win some, lose some" was really the message. The fun part was the teamwork, the friendships, the mishaps, the errors. I remember throwing the ball over the backstop. Everyone laughed, including me.

Our sponsors were usually a tire company, or if you were lucky enough, the ice cream place. Winning the game could only be topped by the amount of sprinkles on the vanilla chocolate twist you got after. Now, when I think back on Little League, the first memory is that of my dad, Mr. Roberts, and Mr. Cavanagh, and the lesson to have fun and keep my eye on the glove. My second is that of the friendships I made, that I still have today with my teammates. The third, and maybe most important, is the sprinkles. What would life be without them?

# Life Before Cell Phones

Once upon a time, there was life before cell phones. I remember we always had one phone in our home, just like most, and it was stationed in the busiest room of the house. In the Leo home, that would be the kitchen, of course. An annual upgrade to the "rotary dial" was a longer cord that reached to the dining room. If my mom or dad was on the phone, kids were always running in and out of rooms, ducking under the cord, stepping over it, or getting tangled in it. Inevitably, I would use it as a way to slow down my sisters who were chasing me, with the slingshot pull. There was also a thing called a busy signal on the rotary dial phones. It just meant that you would yell, "C'mon...get off the phone" repeatedly. There was also no call-waiting, answering machines, caller ID, voice mail, or call-forwarding. So if you were expecting an important one, you simply didn't leave the house. Because there was one phone, it would always be easy to find one of my sisters. All you had to do was trace the cord from the wall to the bathroom with the door closed. If the phone rang during dinner, you simply did not answer it. My dad would yell, "Who in their right mind would call during supper!" Dinnertime was family time and the phone took a back seat, no matter who it was or what they wanted. If it was really important, they would have stopped over.

Then there were the pay phones...good Lord, the payphones. I can remember getting a "calling card" with 97 numbers to type in after dialing the number and getting five minutes to speak and an annoying lady would come on saying I had 30 seconds to finish my call.

Finally came the cordless phone and cell phone. Good or bad? After watching the woman recently check her cell phone and walk into a fountain in a mall - I am not sure. My dad vowed to never, ever get "one of those things," stating firmly, "Why would anyone need one?"

Of course today, I can check the weather on my smartphone, speed dial my best friends, text "Happy Birthday" to someone in Cleveland, send a smile to my aunt in Virginia, poke a classmate on Facebook, and instant message a picture of me in Connecticut to my friend in Switzerland. I can Skype my buddy in New Orleans, listen to Louis Armstrong while I'm running on a treadmill, and watch a YouTube video of the Black Eyed Peas perform their halftime show at the Super Bowl. I can also call my dad, who answers the cell phone he was never going to get. It is ironic that his ringtone is that of the old rotary dial and I smile every time he gets a call.

Life before cell phones was slower, but technology and progress have opened up a world and allowed us to reach others faster. Good or bad? I'm not sure. I just know that recently at work, I was on the landline, listening to a conference call on speakerphone, while talking on my cell phone, while typing an email.

# Siberian Stroll

On Sunday, after a friend and I took a ten-mile bicycle ride, I decided to take my crazy dog for a walk at Mount Hope Reservoir. It was a beautiful fall day, with the leaves changing, and the water sparkling. It had to be one of the most serene, picturesque days of the year. My dog's name is Louis Armstrong (yes, that's his official name). It's so funny to see his family tree: Ksiyuh Tannana enai Galena, Shanya Kaylee Gdoka, Sitka Selawik Noorvik, Notashia Nikita Blue Paw, then *Louis Armstrong Leo*. I find it funny, but he is not amused by it and tells me all of the other dogs in the neighborhood make fun of him.

Anyway, Louie properly marked every one of the 547 trees at Mount Hope Reservoir. Dogs obviously have a never-ending supply of fluid. I had forgotten the hills on the trail and being pulled by a purebred Siberian Husky down some of them made it very entertaining for both of us. I fell, he licked, I fell. We walked all the way around the thing. Yes, it's bigger than I remembered and once you get pretty far, you're not really sure if going back is shorter, so you keep going. I must have gone off the trail because I came upon a sign that said, "If you're at this sign, you've gone too far," so I took a left and found a bridge and made it back safely. When we got in the car, we both had to roll the window down, pant, and stick our heads out. Again, the other drivers looked at us like we were crazy.

When I got home and looked in my book of quotes, I found this one by Albert Camus: ""Do not walk in front of me, for I will not follow you. Do not walk behind me, for I will not lead you.

Rather, walk beside me, and be my friend." I patted Louie on the head, then sent my friend Brownie a text saying, "Thanks for the great ride today buddy." Louie and I both took a nap, listening to *Linus & Lucy*, after a bowl of chili and a bone. Life made sense today.

# Weddings – New Orleans-Style

What do Swamp Thing, a 6'4" German woman, a cab-driving nun, a dog with painted toenails, and I have in common, you might ask? This weekend marked the 25th anniversary of my falling in love with my favorite city, New Orleans. My best buddy, Mitchell Player, the resident upright bass player at the famed Preservation Hall, invited me to his wedding. In true musician fashion, Mitchell forgot to inform me until I arrived that I was actually standing up for him in the wedding. Because his bride's family is from Germany, I was paired with a 6'4" German maid of honor who asked, no – rather, told me, that I would be walking the aisle with her, as she picked me up and deposited me next to her in the procession. "You make good date. Don't make any mistakes," she ordered. I happily obliged. During the exchange of vows in the beautiful and emotional ceremony which was held right inside jazz's greatest living venue, I peered out of the corner of my eye to find a bright green person dressed as Swamp Thing with seaweed covering all of the appropriate places making gurgling noises. A cab pulled up to let out a guest and I noticed the driver was a nun smoking a cigar. The passenger in the back was a raggedy golden retriever, with bright red-painted toenails. Ah, New Orleans, my second home.

My friend Don and his family accompanied me to the wedding and we celebrated their family vacation together. One of the many highlights was our dinner of crawfish etouffee and broiled oysters, where no cell phones were allowed. My observation was "Why would anyone need a cell phone when everyone you love is right at the table?" These people are that kind of a family: caring, kind, in tune with each other, and close. As Jimmy Buffet, Kiss, and the Black Keys performed free in celebration of the Final Four, it was our pleasure to instead enjoy traditional jazz from some of my greatest icons - Leroy Jones, Amanda Shaw, and Shannon Powell. Seeing Kiss, with or without make-up, took a back seat.

To my great friend and his new bride - an amazing ceremony. Mitchell served as the YMCA's music director, after Hurricane Katrina, in our Rome branch. To Don and his family, thank you for being such special people and allowing me to spend time with you. To the 6'4" German woman - "I do what you say." To Swamp Thing - "Exit-stage right" (Get out of the window. There's a wedding going on!).

# The Lost Boys

The story begins…It is the summer of 1977 and two thirteen year old boys go fishing, only to find themselves desperately lost and scared.

Wait. Let me begin again. I recently received an email from Matt, my lifelong friend, asking me to join a network of classmates for next year's 30th class reunion of Oneida High School. The email reminded me of back when we were both 13 years old and we were dropped off at Squashalong Creek (who knows how to actually spell that name and whether it was "Crick" or "Creek") to go fishing on a summer evening.

My recollection is that Matt's dad was going to pick us up at some designated location, but neither Matt nor I remember exactly where that was. We walked along the creek, with poles in hand and bobbers dangling. In those days, it was okay for two young boys to go fishing alone, but as darkness approached, I mean the kind of darkness you get in the woods, things got a little scary. We walked and walked and it was pitch black and we had no idea where we were. Every tree branch that creaked and every night sound we heard of course "must be a bear!" We were convinced it was a large animal, or monster, lurking in the woods ready to snatch us. Several hours later, we magically appeared at Carl's Drug Store in the North Side Shopping Center, happy as could be. We were a little concerned (but not much) that Matt's dad didn't appear to find us. But, oh well, we'd found civilization and escaped the monster on the tracks.

As luck would have it, my Aunt Laura happened to be shopping at Carl's just before they closed at 9:30. We asked her for a ride home to my mom and dad's house on Broad Street near Allen Park and she gladly obliged. Upon arrival in the driveway, we looked around and could not see anyone. No parents, no kids; door wide open and the scanner on. "WE ARE SEARCHING FOR TWO MISSING BOYS LOST IN THE DURHAMVILLE AREA…SEARCH AND RESCUE TEAMS DISPATCHED." German Shepherds were sent out to sniff the trail, State Police were en route, and I think one of my t-shirts was used as a lure for the bloodhounds to find us. Of course, Matt's comment was "Wow, I can't believe two kids are missing" and my revolutionary idea was to question, "Should we help look for them?" Shortly, one of our neighbors came into the house and informed us everyone was looking for us and his wife, in fact, had gone down to St. Patrick's Church and awakened the nuns to ask them to pray for our safe return. My dad backed out and hit a tree in the yard in his haste to find Matt and me. Matt and I innocently wondered what all the commotion was about. We had not been abducted by aliens (to our knowledge), and we were not missing. We were in Carl's Drugs patiently waiting for Aunt Laura to pick up her toothpaste.

Today, life is different. Ironically, I am working as the YMCA CEO with the National Center for Missing & Exploited Children to implement a statewide coalition to improve safety and training to prevent abductions. Matt and I often joke about our episode. When we tell the story now, however, there was no bear and no monster. "Must've been the wind…"

# How to Stretch a Dollar

In the mid -1980s, while in college, it was a common practice to spend your spring break in the South, away from long, cruel winters in Cortland, NY. As did many college kids from all over the country, I finally broke down after three years of abstinence to take the annual pilgrimage to the beaches of America's southeast. Please remember, at that time, Fort Lauderdale was the pinnacle of existence for a college student. It was a chance to take a break from the paper writing, homework, reading, tests, and more tests, and to look for girls, of course. For the first three years of my college career, I went home to Oneida and ate Mom's home cooking, slept in my old bed, and caught up with friends during their break. But in 1986, my senior year, it was time to fly the coop.

John Ready, my old friend and large guy, and two other larger guys, and I planned our excursion. John is 6 feet tall, the two others were both 6'5". We took the only available car of ours capable of making the trip, a Volkswagen Rabbit. We left Cortland, each having no more than $65.00 in our pockets. Yes, that is $65.00 for a week. Eric brought cans of tuna; Bill brought bread, and I brought one apple. John brought tanning lotion with a sun block rating that might even be considered illegal. Our goal was to head to Myrtle Beach and enjoy some sun and some fun. I believed $65.00 was plenty; we all did. We had calculated the gas and because the Rabbit was so efficient, we would be fine. John offered to drive first and as we were packing the car, he put all of our trip's cassette tapes on the roof of the car. The car was a standard, of course, and John, having never previously driven a stick shift, hopped the car all the way down the Thruway. At about the Albany point we realized the cassettes didn't make the trip and miles of tape were trailing us all along the Mohawk Valley. There went my Cars tape, my REO Speedwagon tape, my Journey tape, and my Supertramp tape.

Things were smooth until we reached Myrtle Beach, where the temperature was a whopping 62 degrees. This would not suffice for a spring break, and neither would the average age of its inhabitants. On we went. Georgia looked relatively satisfying until we reached Savannah, where there were no convenience stores to be found anywhere. Temperature: 71; keep going. We pulled into Jacksonville, with a collective, "This is more like it!" Sunny and 84. Keep going was the vote; still too cold. And, anyway, who goes to Jacksonville for Spring Break?

Our new destination: Daytona Beach. It would have been nice if someone had told us it was Bike Week in Daytona, but we settled there at the Surf Echo Motel. Its "luxury" room with amenities such as a bathroom and lights cost us a collective $15.00 per night. We underestimated our funds and came to the conclusion that we could stay two nights, sleep on the beach two nights, and head back a day early. In 1986, for college kids, this was considered deep logic. "On the Dark Side" could be heard blaring from John Cafferty & the Beaver Brown Band as he was our entertainment for the week on a regular gig in Daytona Beach, just outside our hotel.

The first night we spent on the beach resulted in us being tapped on the shoulder by the local law enforcement, stating, "You can't sleep here," and my replying, "Here, Officer? Or anywhere on the beach?" That did not go over too well, so we were forced back to the Surf Echo. With dwindling funds, we decided it was time to head home. As we walked toward the Holiday Inn, I saw a small crowd gathering and asked what was going on. "They're filming an episode of *As the World Turns*," the gentleman said.

I peeked in and was grabbed by a man with a walkie-talkie, who said in his microphone, "I've got a kid." He asked me if I would like to make $200 and as I picked up my sand-filled jaw from the ground, I gasped for air and said, "Of course!" I was instructed to walk around the Holiday Inn pool, holding a girl's hand and run off to the beach with her. Having done so, the man handled me ten $20.00 bills and said, "Thanks, you did great." Not knowing what I just did and having never seen *As The World Turns*, the only thought that crossed my mind was, "We get to stay two more days!"

Later that semester, the stroke of luck long since forgotten, I received a call from an old classmate who was going to school in Rochester. She said, "Quick, turn on the TV; you're on *As the World Turns!!!*"

Of course my dorm room TV didn't get cable, so I had to throw the lampshade that we had copper-wired into a MacGyver antenna onto the roof quickly. By the time I was able to get the channel tuned, it was gone. I only wish I could stretch $65 into a vacation again. Today, it wouldn't cover the tolls.

# The Early Bird

Both the curse and the blessing that has been bestowed on me by my dad has been the necessity to be early for everything I do. The blessing is that I am never late, and always early. My dad considers tardiness a clear sign of disrespect and a lack of consideration for others, and I agree. He is notorious for setting a time to leave for something and if you are not there by the designated time, he is gone. No hard feelings; he is just gone. What that teaches me (and everyone else, for that matter who wants to go fishing with him), is that you'd better be there, and you'd better be early. This lesson to me has been invaluable in my life, my career, and my commitments.

The curse is that I am always too early. I have been the first person to attend a YMCA conference in San Francisco. Of the 647 attendees for the conference, one would think a San Francisco-based person would beat me there. Alas, no such luck. Traveling 3,000 miles, checking into a hotel the night before, waking up early, getting a cab to the hotel, and arriving first in line (usually as the registration table is being set up, I am asked to help), is a common practice. I have been shopping in Wal-Mart while the cleaning crew is in and the aisles are roped off for most of the departments. Though this sometimes deters my search for a tube of toothpaste, I find a way to sneak under the rope. Sometimes when I wear a tie on a particular day, the cleaning crew mistakes me for an out-of-state supervisor and lobbies me for a pay raise. I have also arrived early enough to be handed a blue apron and a nametag.

When I went to Cortland State my first year, I arrived so early (about a week), that I was given the RA job. Usually, first-year students are not given this role, but because one of the RAs decided to transfer during orientation and the alternates list was depleted, and I happened to be there, guess who got the job. When I am the Director on Duty on some Saturday mornings at the Y, my shift starts at 7AM. I arrive at 5, get the building set up, lights on, pool cover off, and wait at the desk for about an hour before anyone arrives. They all know it is not open yet. I find it comforting; my staff and the members find it insane. Sometimes I start projects years in advance and work on them until the time arrives when I feel I am ready. To others, it appears to be "leadership vision;" to me, it's simply my planning time. I do not use an alarm clock as it broke years ago, and my watch battery died right around the same time. I just like the look of the watch. People often ask me what the time is, and I reply, "I'm not sure."

People often contact me and say, "I got an email from you at 4:45 this morning. Are you up at that time?" The question itself is an answer as it would be difficult to type while I'm sleeping although that is when my best work is done (I frequently wake up and write thoughts down). I finally came to the understanding that those who are early get things. I always thought it was because I earned a particular job, but now it's clear that if you arrive early, you will be assigned something. I am sure there are other people with my syndrome and they too suffer from "Early-itis." It can be a terrible challenge. It's lonely; I can tell you that. The only thing I'd really like to be late for is my own funeral.

# "Down, Boy"

Everyone's got a "most embarrassing moment" story, but few will share. It's confession time. Well, a bunch of years ago, I met a terrific girl when I was living in Syracuse. We had just met and I asked her on a date. Unfortunately, she was moving to Colorado the next morning. We stayed in touch for a few months, then on my birthday she sent me a plane ticket to visit her. I flew in, rented a car, and found a nice hotel just outside of Colorado Springs. I remember asking the hotel receptionist where Pike's Peak was and she just pointed up. Nancy gave me directions and after cleaning up, I drove out to her sister and brother-in-law's house where she was staying to pick her up for a nice, quiet dinner at a restaurant of her choice.

With rose in hand, I walked up their sidewalk: "Knock, knock, knock" on the solid wooden door. No one responded, but I could hear a dog bark as if to say, "I don't know this guy." Then I heard a faint "C'mon in; we're in the back." I opened the door and a big, burly boxer jumped up and put his two mittens of paws on my shoulders. I said "Down!" (I'm a dog guy and I know the commands.) The big boy took a step back, walked around in three circles, collapsed on the floor, and was dead as a doorknob. Yes, before the family had even arrived at the door. I wasn't sure what to do or say. Nancy, her sister, brother-in-law, and their kids came out and just looked on the floor, then at me. I cannot believe I actually said this but the words came out and I couldn't stop them: "Does he always do this?" as foam was starting to form at his mouth.

The sister collected the kids and took them into the kitchen for a "family counseling session." I could hear whispers from little voices, "What's wrong with Duke?" I thought, "Oh, God, please tell me the dog's name isn't Duke."

The brother-in-law said, "What happened?" I said, "Uh, er, I walked in when you said to come in." "Please tell me Duke was old and sick," I begged. I think he sort of felt sorry for me.

He said, "I don't know. He is, um, was, only two...maybe boxers are known for heart attacks." He went in with the family. I stood in the living room for what seemed like hours, nervously scanning the dozens of wall photos of Duke with the kids, Duke with Grandma, Duke with Mom and Dad, and some of Duke alone. One was labeled "Best Friend." Oh God, Part II.

We spent the next few hours digging a hole in the back yard. We gave Duke a proper burial. I offered my coat as a wrap. It was not necessary. I was asked to say the prayer. I almost started with "Yea, though I walk through the valley of the shadow..." and then thought better.

Whatever happened to Nancy, you might ask...She forgave me. Her sister did not.

If you see her, know anyone who knows her, know a friend of a cousin who has met her, know people that have dogs named Duke... please pass along my heartfelt apologies; I swear, I just knocked.

# The Car Wash

One spring day, I needed to get my car washed. It was one of those carwashes where you drive up, put in your money, and the bay door opens slowly, you pull in, the door closes behind you, and the wash begins. Well...I did put in my money, the door did, in fact, open, I did pull in, and the wash began as it should have.

First, the rinse cycle came. Next, a coat of blue, red, and purple foam covered the car and the windshield, and lathered the '05 Honda like a rainbow. Then, it just stopped. As I waited for the rinse cycle to begin, silence. "Drip, drip, drip" was all I heard. So, I was in my car covered in soap, and the wash just stopped.

After a little panic, my plan was to get out of the car and see what the problem was. Springtime in central New York can be a mixed bag of weather. I had a suit on and it was freezing. I was afraid that as soon as I got out of the car, the wash would start and I would be covered in rainbow, soapy water. Didn't happen. I braved the risk and exited the driver's seat, looked around, and couldn't find any way to either get the thing going or open the electric doors. I was trapped in the car wash with no way to get out. "Ah, my cell phone," I thought cleverly. Of course I should have known that in a carwash, there would be no reception, and I had no bars. I threw the phone on the passenger's seat as I sat in disgust. Again, I would like to add that the doors to the bays were down and shut. But I had a brilliant idea. My goal was to pry open the back door, get out of the wash, and re-pay for the wash to see if it would open the doors again.

Imagine trying to pry your garage door at home open by hand…well, this is what I did, suit and all. I got it about three feet off the ground, but it kept dropping back down, so I found a tube, the kind used for mailing posters, in the garbage can and propped the door up. I got down on my stomach, praying aloud that the door would not come crashing down on me, sawing me in half like a magician's assistant. I slithered under the door like a snake and the tube broke and the door shut. But "Ha!" I was outside. I reached into my pocket and found that I only had a $20.00 bill. This particular wash did not take $20.00 bills. Of course it didn't.

I walked to the store about a half a mile away, forgot that my cell phone was in the car (again, locked in), and got change for the $20. So I could not call anyone, my phone was in my car, and my car was in a car wash. I walked the half-mile back to the car wash and deposited the minimum $10.00 into the machine and waited for the door to rise. To my disbelief, the wash started again, with my car locked in the bay, and me outside. When the wash was done, I sprinted around the front of the wash, hoping desperately to see the door open. It did. I ran to the driver's side, jumped in the car, started it, and the door closed again. Right back where I'd started. This time, at least the car was clean. Back to the tube, and yes, it was crushed, but still sturdy. Let the crawling and sprawling recommence! Retracing my steps, I crawled out again and deposited the money for two washes this time. The wash began. I ran to the front, jumped in the car, washed my car for the third and fourth times, and drove out the front.

Yes, I was covered in soapy water; I had lost $20, and I'd washed my car four times. As I drove away, mixed in with the soapy water were tears of laughter. I was the only one who knew my adventure, until now.

# The Angel

I think everyone feels that their mom is one of the most important people in their lives. I hear people refer to their mom as a best friend and nurturer, always with thanks and appreciation. When I think of my mom, I always think of the simplicity with which she views life. Mom never says anything bad about anyone and always tries to look at the positive side of life. She enjoys the little things, the things that others take for granted. It's not uncommon for her to create baskets of items for needy children at elementary schools, help with causes for kids, or donate money to this effort or that need. By trade, she was a teaching assistant at an elementary school, and worked in the lunch room at our high school. In an era when lunch ladies were not treated very well or given much respect by kids, everyone loved my mom. After she retired, she just continued to give and give.

Mom's heritage is English, Irish, German, and French, while my dad is full Italian. And can she cook! Chicken riggies, or what we called "stove pipes," were my favorite dish. The sauce came from Dad's garden and since his tomatoes created the sauce, he felt ownership in trying out the meatballs before dinner was ready. She would shoo him out of the kitchen often, hitting his hand with the wooden spatula. Mom was supportive of my sisters and their things. She would sit through hours of my sister Terri's dance recitals. These recitals always strategically placed the kids in the very beginning and the very end so that the audience would have to stay for the whole thing. Dad and I would always drive separately so that he and I could sneak away during the intermission. "Hank Jr.'s not feeling too well, might have to take him to the house."

Mom would reply, "Okay, but make sure you're back for the finale. Terri's coming out at 9:45 again." We would both grumble a little, then smile. Mom was the neighborhood hostess to my friends. Everyone met at the Leo home for family meals. We grew up right across from the park and would raid the fridge on more than one occasion. When Dad came home from work and wanted to know where all of the cheese was, she would defend me: "Hank, he's a growing boy and needs his calcium. Get out of the fridge or you'll ruin your appetite."

Every Sunday, for the past twenty years or so, Mom and Dad have gone to the regional market. They will find trinkets, household items, gifts for birthday presents, or find things that others have put them on the lookout for. They stop on the way home at garage sales and usually at a local diner to grab a bite to eat. It's their time to share and to be with each other. Sometimes I will go to the market on my own and bump into Mom. She will always stop and say, "I got this for Louie," and take out a big bone from a paper bag. She knows how much my dog means to me.

Mom has a special way about her, the way I imagine an angel would have. She looks after people, cares, and comforts them. She's sympathetic to everyone's needs, shares in their grief when they need it, and in their happiness when they need that too. I imagine an angel to be the one you go to when you need to be held and told everything is going to be okay. The angel needs to be strong and take the brunt of the anxiety and angst to make you feel better. The angel needs to be the rock you rely on and hold out a wing to shelter you. The angel needs to bow their head and pray for you, to keep you safe.

My mom, like so many other moms, is truly an angel, never giving in to a burden and taking it on her shoulders to share my load. How do you thank someone for that? Words don't seem enough.

# What Scares Me

I was watching a scary movie this week and tried to remember things that scared me as a kid and thought I would share. Bats, spiders, snakes, worms - no problem. But these?

Here you go, the Top 25:

- Clowns…they were big, orange, and had gigantic feet. They looked like creepy old guys and I didn't trust them.

- Under the bed…it was dark and if your arm or foot dangled off the edge it was fair game for the monster.

- In the closet…no way was I opening that door at night.

- Owls…their heads spun all the way around - and they had eyes like Marty Feldman.

- The flying monkeys from Wizard of Oz

- Tie between the Wicked Witch of the West and the Old Maid from a card deck. Witch wins by a nose.

- The down escalator. Where did those steps lead…the monster at the bottom ate the steps; I was next.

- Old portraits. I swear the eyes followed me wherever I went in the room.

- Dueling Banjos…see "Deliverance."

- Maude

- Noises at night coming from the basement

- Noises at night coming from the roof

- Noises at night coming from me

- Ironing (Okay, that's an adult one.)

- The Whirly Bird (I flew off it when I was a kid and landed on an Allen Park bench and cut my ear open.)

- The dentist (Still am. Sorry, Dr. Stewart.)

- Snowblowers…there was a finger incident.

- Jarts…there was another incident.

- Darts…I watched a friend have an incident.

- Pickled beets. I thought they were slices of an organ or something.

- The *Night Stalker* with Darren McGavin. Still scary, especially the zombie episode.

- Andre the Giant. He was like 10 feet tall; I was 3 feet tall and we both talked funny.

- When there were hundreds of crows crowing…I always thought they were planning an aerial attack on me.

- Lasagna…I ran into a pan my sister Debbie was carrying and split my head open.

- Forks scraping a plate. I don't know why, it was just scary.

# The Barber Shop

So...the other day, I decided to go to the barbershop to get a haircut, instead of going to my usual hair salon. I don't know when guys started going to salons instead of barbershops; I just know I switched at some point, for some reason, and I don't know why. Anyway, when you walk into the barber's, you get that instant smell of talc, after shave, powder, and camaraderie you just cannot find anywhere else in the world. There is always a guy already sitting in the chair, no matter what time you get there. The chair, of course, is from the 1920s and hasn't been upgraded in its 90-year history, but there would be no need for that. It turns, swivels and gets pumped up and down by a handle. This type of mechanical genius cannot be found in a salon. The room has all of the amenities: a coat rack, chairs, and seat. That is all one needs.

As you wait your turn, you read the paper. Usually, you are reading a paper from a few days ago, but that doesn't really matter. There are always a few other guys sitting there as well who have already read the paper and can tell you anything you want to know. "What do you think of that Obama guy?" is mumbled from a corner. The question is delivered as if he were just elected yesterday. "See the Yanks last night?" is answered in response. "Damn taxes..." comes from near the coat rack. I am next up on the imaginary list of rank and order and head to the chair. No one really communicates who is next; we just internally know the order. No one knows the prices, either. They are implied. In the salon, there is a host of choices. In barbershops, it is a haircut or no haircut. You could just sit there and no one would care.

The chair is brushed off with a towel, the handle lowers the seat; you jump in and on goes the plastic cape. It is tightened around your neck with something. No one knows for sure what it is because we have never seen it. "What'll it be today?" asks the master.

"The usual," I say. It is possible I haven't been in the "chair" in ten years, but he knows what "the usual" is. In barber lingo, it refers to "one on the sides and back, trim up what's left," but of course, he knows that. Out come the clippers and the barber wields it like a Ginsu Knife, slicing and dicing the sides and back, trimming sideburns, around the ears. "Catch any of the game last night?" he begins. "Tough one," I reply.

The game could mean baseball, basketball, football, or even an Olympic event. It never means soccer, tennis, racquetball, or swimming. And, if you answer "tough one," you'll always be right. It is also true that the more you talk, the more hair is cut. This can be dangerous for a guy like me. So, I stick to short answers. Out come the scissors. CLIP, CLIP, CLIP, CLIP...done. Next is the shaving of the little hairs: the nose, the ears, and correcting any mistakes made with the Ginsu.

Last, out comes the brush. It looks like the brush the home plate umpire uses to dust off the plate in between innings and may even be the same one. That is used to get all of the hairs off your neck and send you on your way. The chair is spun around like a top and you are now facing the mirror. He questions "Good?" You nod, of course. I have never heard anyone say, "No, that wasn't what I had in mind." You're a guy; you'd better like it because another guy did it. And a bunch of other guys are watching you. The magic cape is removed and snapped like a matador in a bullring. "Next!"

# Things Have Changed Since I Was a Kid

Over the weekend, I went to a Little League game and was thinking back to when I played and how much things have changed. I was talking to the guy next to me and commented, "I remember when finding 17 other kids to play baseball at a park was easy." No parents, no coaches, no supervision. If there weren't enough on some days, we simply created "ghost men," who ran for our teams. Allen Park (turned sideways) was Yankee Stadium, Shea Stadium, Three Rivers...you name it. Mom's broomstick was the bat and, well, tennis balls were the baseballs. Scott played short, Bobby played third and Tommy played first. I always pitched. To hit a homerun, you had to bat opposite handed because the regular way was just too easy. Bobby always tried to hit like Lou Pinella, but of course Lou never hit homeruns...neither did Bobby.

It was hard to limit kickball games to 20 or 30 kids and when it was your turn "up," looking out at the sea of kids, you thought, "Where could I possibly kick it without it getting caught?" When one of the neighborhood legends was "up" at Allen Park, there would be about a dozen kids in my parents' yard, daring them to kick it that far from the big tree near the water fountain. Sometimes what seemed like a thousand or more would watch a tournament in bleachers or lawn chairs. Our "Turkey Bowl" on Thanksgiving Day at the high school was more attended than any Lions game in Detroit.

As kids, our curfew was the streetlights. Our moms called our names, not our cell phones. We played outside with friends, not online. If we didn't eat what our moms cooked, then we didn't eat.

Sanitizer didn't exist, but you COULD get your mouth washed out with soap. We rode our bikes without helmets and getting dirty was OK. The neighbors cared as much about me as my parents did.

Time was told by the streetlights: "on" meant it was time to go home. "Starting to come on" meant another 15 minutes. Kick-the-Can was played by 40 or 50 kids. Basketball games of "Rochester" or "21" or "Horse" became very creative. "Off the backboard, through the legs, around the back, opposite-hand, with eyes closed." The park pavilion was where you hand-painted your name. The "Spike Tree" in Allen Park was where you climbed to hide during "TV Tag." You only prayed during "Red Rover" that the big kid didn't come barreling through. Games of "Spud" were awesome: whip the ball up, everyone runs - when you catch it, they have to stop and you can chuck it at them to get the "out." If they caught it, you were out. Simple, but free and no need for training. Any hill was a bike jump. Any stick was a bat. Nikes weren't necessary - the more colorful the Chuck Taylors, the better. Striped socks were cool. Hats backwards meant you were too. Being a radical meant you went to see *Jaws* when you were under 18 without your parent knowing it. Kindle was what you looked for to start the fireplace for the marshmallows, not what you used to read.

It's a shame that because of all of the craziness in the world, those days are distant memories. We didn't need "SIM" anything. It was real. We didn't need to text; you just had to call one kid and tell him what time we were playing, and he called the next, and she called the next. Before too long, you had a couple dozen; no "Droids" necessary. Getting 18 kids to play baseball in the park was a modern day "flash mob." However, as I am typing this, I have my iPod in my car, my Blackberry next to me, and I'm using email all day. Hypocrite, I know. I just miss it sometimes.

# How We Talked Back In the Day

In the world of texting, abbreviating, instant messaging, and using all kinds of crazy sayings that shorten the verbiage but get the point across, it is important to look back on where we have come from and how we have grown since the days of technology. I was at the store the other day and heard two mid-forties women talking in line behind me. One said, "No way Jose," and the other responded, "Way." It reminded me of a thousand sayings we all used to spew from our mouths "back in the day." It seems like I might always have been a little step behind the others, because I still use some of them. Here are my Top 21. And, yes, I'm a dork:

- Don't be such a spaz (Spaz meaning you're freaking out over something not that important.)

- Psyche! (Yes, I've tricked you. "I just dropped your cell phone in the toilet...psyche!")

- "Goodnight, John-Boy." (I used this one often when we were at a camp or a conference and it was lights-out time.)

- "You da Man" (Every guy who plays golf still says this, but you have to wait until exactly when the guy strikes the ball on his drive.)

- "That's the bomb." (Lasted about a year and never made sense, like "I love that dress - that's the bomb!" and you can't use it at an airport.)

- "Bogus" (Everything was, or it was just cool to say it. The people saying it weren't very bright. Example: "22 + 22 =44? That sounds bogus.")

- "Bummer" (Sorry, man, as in: "Wow, you really got stuck in a car wash? Bummer...")

- "Cool beans" and "easy breezy" (A nice girl would say this when something good happened to her.)

- "Dang!" "Oh Snap!" and "Shut the front door." (Shows that you are really irritated, but without actually swearing.)

- "Nice!" (As when Don Moore or John Little makes a great shot in Saturday morning Y basketball.)

- "Sweet!" (See "Nice.")

- "Gag me with a spoon." (From every girl I graduated with when I asked her out.)

- "Jump yer bones" (What I would say to make the girls say, "Gag me with a spoon.")

- "Jonesin' (As in, "I really need something right now. I'm Jonesin' for a Fluffernutter sandwich.")

- "Let's blow this taco stand." (I don't even think there was one in Oneida then, but it was still funny.)

- "Nanoo, Nanoo" (Not sure why I really wanted to be like Mork, but that's how we greeted people, very briefly. I also threw an egg up in the air and said, "Fly and be free!")

- "Slap me some skin." (This has been replaced by the high five, then the fist bump; I feel it will make an eventual comeback.)

- "Take a chill pill!" (Pretty much the same as, "Don't be such a spaz," but with more authority and conviction - relax!)

- "Word" ("I agree." You didn't really believe them, but you wanted to sound cool by saying you did: "You read the Bible? Word!")

- And my favorite, the one that stands the test of time, "Hubba Hubba" (It's a totally awesome, rad saying that's off-the-hook. Try it on your spouse and see what happens.)

# Just One of the Girls

The best part of being the only boy in the family and having three sisters is that you don't get any hand-me-downs. The worst part is having to shovel the driveway, mow the lawn, take the garbage out, and be the last one to use the bathroom. Finding strings of hair, little scrunchy things, hundreds of barrettes, and a host of feminine products strewn across the only shower in our house made me want to stay as far away from home on a daily basis as possible. The constantly-running hairdryer, phone cord going from the kitchen to the closed bathroom door, endless array of dolls and doll clothes, posters of Andy Gibb and Shawn Cassidy, Teen Beat magazines, and VHS tapes of Flash Dance laying around nearly hospitalized me. It's no wonder when my dad would ask me if I wanted to go out in the yard and pick nightcrawlers, I jumped out at the chance. The dirtier the job, the better.

I think I terrorized my younger sister. I used to play the Incredible Hulk when she and her friends were at the house and left to my care in my parents' absence. I used to growl and pick them up and throw them on the couch or rug. I think I also spiked their peanut butter and jelly sandwiches with hot sauce. It was funny to me at the time, but now I think of how cruel it was to pretend I was a big green monster with a propensity to watch my siblings sweat while eating lunch. Eventually, my older sisters married, moved out of the house and to a different state. My oldest sister moved to Germany and my middle sister moved to Virginia. I couldn't be happier that the bathroom was finally available. Now the room could be filled with Jovan Musk, a Bic razor, Brylcreem, and Desenex Foot Powder - the way a real men's room should be. Dolls were replaced by G.I. Joes. Andy Gibb and Shawn Cassidy were torn down and shredded; Hank Aaron and Tom Seaver fit nicely in their place. The record player blasted REO Speedwagon's *Ridin' the Storm Out*. Ah, freedom at last.

I grew up surrounded by women. I learned the habits, knew the importance of shopping, translated gossip to my guy friends, and figured out early the vital necessity of shoe selection. I also understood mood swings, voice inflections, unstoppable chocolate cravings, and body language. I learned how to sew, how to fold socks, how to make pancakes, and that bras shouldn't be used as slingshots. On the more practical side, I learned how to detect if someone is lying, tell someone when I'm mad or sad instead of keeping it in, and give someone space when they need it. In an era where guys were supposed to be the Marlboro Man and women were supposed to be Daisy Duke, I was lucky. I had a dad and mom that taught me how to be strong, and three sisters who taught me that the best strength isn't physical.

# The Legend of St. Pat's Gym

Any kid who grew up in Oneida in my era knows of the rite of passage to teen years by attending the dances in the St. Patrick's Church gym. Of course, this was the late '70s and early '80s. Dances were the places where you were destined to build up enough nerve to ask that one girl to dance with you. This is not to be confused with the roller skating days at the Kallet Theater. They didn't officially count because there was athleticism involved and the roller skating music was awful. You see, when it came to St. Pat's dances, EVERYONE waited anxiously for Friday night to come. I can remember walking down the stairs to the church kitchen where everyone put their coats and hung out until the doors opened. As soon as they did, you could barely see into the gym because it was pitch black with the exception of the disco ball hanging from the ceiling.

There was a table where Spad and Coach sat and spun tunes all night. They were awesome. All of the guys would be on the right-hand side and all of the girls on the left. Chairs lined the perimeter which allowed for "scoping" across the court and chaperones with flashlights dictated the height of the guys' hands on their dance partners. It paid to be a short guy. In the beginning of the night, you would always hear "Raise a Little Hell" by Trooper; "Take the Money and Run" by Steve Miller; "You Shook Me All Night Long" by AC/DC, of course; and the showstopper "Paradise by the Dashboard Lights." The first half of "Paradise" is slow, so if you asked a girl to dance with you - as soon as it sped up (you know the part, where the girl says "Ain't no doubt about it, we were doubly blessed…"), all of the guys would abruptly leave their partners on the dance floor, where they would be joined shortly by their girl-friends. Guys just didn't dance then and with good reason.

Of course the gym in St. Pat's now looks much smaller than it did then. The ceiling must have some holes in it from me trying to make a basket over the years. My friend, Ritchie, however, had no such problem. This guy shoots 95% on most every court, but in the St. Pat's gym, he shot 100%. In a dozen years or so, I never saw him miss a basket. Anyway, back to the dances.

I would always go with a group of friends and meet other groups of friends there. We had to get prepared - make sure the hair was perfect (parted in the middle, feathered back), then wear a hat over it, sometimes a cowboy hat. I still to this day am not sure why, but alas, not much of what we did made sense. At the end of the night it was time for "Freebird" by Lynyrd Skynyrd. Again, a slow song that turns fast. I always looked for Kim Viens to ask her to dance, but chickened out a hundred times. She was beautiful; I was, well…not. It's hard today to imagine dancing to "Stairway to Heaven," but it was the headliner and we loved it.

All the kids walked to the dance and we walked home after. There was no need to worry, because we would head up to Carroll's (now Burger King, of course), or to Pepi's Pizza. We would laugh and talk about which girl said what to us, how it made us feel, whether we thought she "liked us or not," and who we were going to ask to dance at the next one. Thank God they created the Sadie Hawkins dance, because we, the guys, could avoid the horror of having to do the asking. Ah, the teen years - lessons in courage, strength, failure, friendships, self-esteem, humility, seduction, rejection, and utter stupidity – not unlike the adult years.

# Father's Day

Thinking about Father's Day this year is like watching my life flash before my eyes. My first clear memory is a collage of days of playing catch on my front lawn with my dad. He was a catcher and I was a pitcher. Dad's hero was Yogi Berra. He looked like him and played like him, although I think Dad was actually a bit taller. I would pitch to my dad and he would always encourage me. He'd tell me to throw to the glove and not take my eyes off it. Metaphorically, 40 years later, I try never to take my "eyes off the ball" or, in other words, never take my focus off the goal.

Dad knew I had two favorite players as a kid. I loved Hank Aaron and I loved the Mets and Lee Mazzilli at the time. Dad thought so much of making my dreams come true, he took me to old Jerry Park in Montreal to see the Braves play the Expos. Of course, Hammerin' Hank hit numbers 703 and 704 that day, on his chase of Babe Ruth's record of 714 homeruns. And we were there. As Hank was getting "hammered" by racists, Dad told me not to pay attention to color as a way of judging people. Forty years later, I have enjoyed a life of great diversity and color has never been a barrier. A couple of years later, he took me to Shea Stadium to see my first Mets game and of course, Lee Mazzilli hit a grand slam to win the game. Magic? Probably not. Most likely, it's God's way of making things right.

You see, I know that a lot of "Juniors" try deliberately to *not* act like their fathers, and to be their own person. To me, every time someone says, "You're just like your father," it is the highest compliment someone can pay me. Emulating my dad does bring some challenges, though. I am the first to arrive anywhere and I get impatient when people are late. I once attended a conference in Los Angeles, a national conference, and was the first one to arrive - even ahead of the California people; 347 people, and I was the first one there. I also get up way too early for no reason. I've finished my day and looked at the clock and it's 10AM on a Sunday. There are many positive things that I have gotten from my dad too. When I make up my mind to do something, I do it. And almost every decision I make is because of common sense. I try to be caring, friendly to everyone I meet, hard working, and supportive of my family, no matter what the circumstances. This was always the theme in my parents' house.

My dad can run anything. Put him in charge, and it gets done. I also learned courage from my dad. I wish I had half of the strength he has. He has respect from everyone who meets him, without ever having to ask for it. What I haven't learned yet is how to fish like him. I have been in the same boat, on the same side. I do the exact same things he does. The results, however, are never the same. Within fifteen minutes, he has his limit and I haven't gotten a bite. Same bait, same water, same technique. His fishing buddies tell me the same happens with them. He always says, "All the fish must be on this side." I gave him a digital camera recently to prove all of those big fish stories. Lately, he's been telling me he forgot to bring the camera. But I know better. When my dad had to get some treatment in Rome a couple of years ago, we drove every day to the doctor's office. I would drop him off to a room filled with patients and people complaining about their conditions and their afflictions saying, "How could this happen to me?" At the end of the day, I would pick him up to go home and everyone in the room would be laughing and telling stories, exchanging Italian recipes. The next day he would bring in food he had cooked for all of them.

I hope everyone, whatever their circumstances, is able to recall what they learned from their dads, too: how to be strong and how to help other people. To me, love and support should happen every day, in every family. Whether the family is a single mom, dad, step-mom, step-dad, or foster parent, something good can be taken away from your time together. Remember what they taught you. Pay attention to the lessons. They had the courage to have you, to bring you into the world, and to raise you, sometimes in difficult circumstances. Return the favor. Be with them during good times and in tough ones. Love them like they love you. Call, write, text, or quietly remember your dad or the one serving as your dad for now; tell him you love him and thank him. It will mean a lot to both of you.

# The Fisherman
## (In Honor of My Dad, Hank Leo Sr.)

5:45 AM, the sun glistens on the cold, calm waters of Oneida Lake.

The boat is loaded and secured to the dock; a single rope steadies the floating salvation.

Coffee brews in the marina, the morning news is shared.

As the Fisherman climbs aboard his mighty metal steed

A grin creases his weathered face. It is time. There is nowhere else he would rather be.

Out to Buoy 107 maybe; Southeastern wind headed this way.

A selection is made from the rows of hand-crafted lures.

"What color are we using today?" asks his son.

Blue, like the water this morning.

Tens of feet of line weave in and out of the waves as the motor gently trolls.

Early tomorrow morning yet another treatment awaits.

The sun will glisten off hospital windows

as he sits for hours in a chair, waiting patiently.

Tens of feet of IV line will weave in and out of those sharing a similar day.

Tubes, needles, drips. There are many places he would rather be.

He remembers that Jesus said, "Follow me and I will make you fishers of men."

His boat was small, his message simple.

Many a man has learned from the Fisherman.

Like the walleye, his "eyeshine" gives him sight

Seeing, not *in* the dark, but *through* it. He reminds his son:

> "Arise early and seize the day.
> Live not for the moment but for the stay.
> Enjoy your friends, the calm, and the peace.
> Let not your approach to a challenge cease.
> Give me a test, a life-threatening chore
> And the Fisherman will show you how to even the score.
> How do I get my limit? you ask.
> 'Denial,' is the answer. It's no easy task.
> I refuse to believe they will not bite
> Just as I refuse to believe my end is in sight.
> Like the fish who takes the hook and the bait
> The Fisherman alone decides his fate.
> The lesson to learn is to never give in.
> Keep casting your rod and your back to the wind."

6:15 AM, like a fly landing on a reed

The line wiggles slightly and bends. Only the Fisherman can feel it.

A jerk and a reel in.

If he dies here today, he is happy.

Though the walleye are few, there is nowhere else he would rather be.

7:12 AM, back to the marina they head, catch in hand.

Told too many times, "You don't have long..."

Too often warned, "The end is close..."

It is not close. Not even close.

He smiles at his son and whispers, "Not today."

# Louie's Diary

I know it is not proper for parents to sneak in and read their children's diaries, but I happened to be curious last night and read my Siberian Husky, Louie's, entry from yesterday. He doesn't know I did it and would be angry if someone told him. Please keep it between us:

5:35 AM   Got woken up by the screaming, flying, black thing again. He flew onto the telephone wire and joined his friends to mock me - a morning ritual.

6:01   Stretched my front legs first, then the back ones, and yawned, all in one motion.

6:09   Dad patted me on the head and said something - no idea, but it sounded like "boy." He still calls me boy and I am 63; he doesn't seem too bright to me.

6:33   Yelled at the big metal thing on wheels that picks up the small, plastic thing once a week, letting him know again this is my house. He didn't seem to care and made a lot of noise anyway.

6:40   Walked around in a circle three times and lay down.

11:00   Squirrel ran by again. Someone told him exactly how long my chain is and he continues to taunt me.

11:18   Walked around in a circle again and lay down.

12:02PM   A two-wheeled thing with a girl on it went by, but she was gone before I could see who it was; woofed.

1:14   Chain got caught on the big rock again; took me three times to figure out what direction to go to make the chain longer, thought to myself, "Apple doesn't fall too far from the tree."

1:15   Watered the bush.

2:08   Smaller metal thing on wheels came again - put Dad's papers in the box; lady driving is on the wrong side as usual.

2:12   Watered the bush, same spot.

2:38   Squirrel walked by this time, calling me a "four-legged fur-ball"; I responded with "Look who's talking!"

2:40   Did my business beside the bush; that should prevent him from trespassing on my property.

2:45   Water break.

2:46   Watered the bush.

2:54   Tried to pull the house closer to the squirrel path; mumbled "Some day..."

3:12   Thought I saw a cute girl drive by. False alarm.

3:14   Cleaned my tail just in case she does come by. Hey, a guy can hope.

3:18   Neighbor yelled at me for what I would consider being friendly. He considered it "loud and obnoxious."

3:49   Group of the flying things went over my head honking; I didn't even look up -didn't want to give them the satisfaction.

4:13   When is Dad coming home?

4:23   "Dad's back!" False alarm, grey metal thing with wheels turned around in driveway; yelled "Loser!"

4:35   Flying thing left white spot on my bush; watered it just in case.

5:12   "Dad's home!" Lick, lick, lick-"Get me off this chain! Where's the food? What's in your pocket? Can I go behind the house? I'd like to water other stuff! Do you know what separation anxiety is? How do I get on Facebook? How long were you gone, a month?"

# Ah, Yes, the '80s

I have, from time to time, reflected on my childhood, but it is time to venture out into the high school and college years, those forgettable '80s. Kim Carnes' raspy "Bette Davis Eyes," Christopher Cross' "Sailing," Kenny Rogers' "Lady," and Air Supply's "The One That You Love" graced the Top 10 in Billboard. Not on my stereo, however. You could walk into my room and hear Clapton, Styx, REO, Foreigner, the Police, Supertramp, Steely Dan and ELO. Of course, as always, you could still hear "Hello Dolly" from Satchmo. (Yes, I was the only guy growing up in the '70s and '80s listening to '40s music.)

I paid no attention to politics. I actually remember thinking The Cold War was called that because it was in Russia (where I thought Siberia was near). I was most likely too busy playing on my Commodore 64 computer or watching *Cheers*. My favorite episode was when Coach was walking across the floor of the bar on his hands and he said to Sam, "Hey Sammy, remember when I used to walk across the dugout on my hands?" Sam replied, "Coach, that wasn't you; that was Johnson!" Then you just heard a crash...priceless. I do remember the Challenger space shuttle exploding, with teacher Christa McAuliffe on board. I sat in my dorm room and gasped as I saw it happen on TV.

In college, I actually took classes in computer language, with the big cards with holes in them and ran them through a mainframe that looked like one of the boilers at the Y. I learned COBAL, FORTRAN and some other acronyms that I do not remember. I do remember that FORTRAN meant "formula translation." Yes,

War Games was front and center. And, I remember that LASER meant "Light amplification stimulated emission of radiation." Useless information, but I remember it. I recall my professor telling me, "You kids really need to learn computer languages; they are going to be 'in' some day." I remember actually saying to my classmates, "Do you think we'll always have to program something? Why can't somebody smarter than us do that and we just use it?" Go figure.

Going to lunch at the student union was basically the same every day: "I'm hungry and I have points on my card; let's eat." My hero then was Alex P. Keaton, the witty Republican Michael J. Fox. I even became an intern for a brokerage firm for a few months. This was not because of my entrepreneurial spirit, but because I thought it would attract girls, just like the one he got to see - the beautiful Tracy Pollan, whom he ended up marrying. I also got to see another one of my childhood crushes, Chelsea Noble. I met her one day at a fundraiser in Syracuse back in the '80s. I was using the men's restroom in a store where she was doing a promotion with her husband Kirk Cameron and she walked in mistakenly. I turned, while going, looked over my shoulder by the door, and she said, "Whoops, sorry..." and put her hand over her eyes. So, my brief brush with stardom happened in a bathroom, with the love of my life.

Sports were pretty awesome. *Miracle on Ice* happened and the world cheered like it was our home team; and it was. Michael Jordan flew through the air. Mike Tyson knocked out everyone within a matter of seconds. I remember the fight he had with Buster Douglas vividly. I remember a bunch of us guys went to see it at a restaurant on Pay per View, and Mike was getting the crud beat out of him - something that never happened. We reached out to the TV and said, "Mike, tag me!"

Wayne Gretzke made hockey fans out of people who didn't even like hockey. It wasn't only sports; it was style and fashion, too. I was looking for a girlfriend who wore leg warmers, shoulder pads, and a jean jacket with big, teased hair. Of course, I was luring them with my "Members Only" jacket. I still to this day do not know what the club was that I belonged to. I remember Halley's Comet, the Yugo, and I wanted to beat up Billy Idol for bragging about dancing with himself. "Oh, oh, oh, oh…" Boom! I also wanted to take on Randy "Macho Man" Savage. I was in love with the short, brown-haired girl from the Bangles; I think her name was Suzanna. Oh, Suzanna! I loved Kristy McNichol for some reason. I thought Kim Carnes was hot and Lita Ford was hotter.

I don't know who shot J.R., but I was a suspect. Hated that show. I loved "St. Elmo's Fire," but never understood who St. Elmo was or why they chose that for the title. Most of the people wrote in my yearbook, "See ya around this summer," a very sentimental message that I would hold close to my heart for eternity.

I could go on and on, but like, oh my God, I'm totally over the '80s.

# Signs You Might Be From Oneida, NY

- You might be from Oneida if your tan is actually wind burn.

- You might be from Oneida if when it turns 40 degrees, it is safe to go to the park and swing without frostbite.

- You might be from Oneida if you've lived here all of your life and you've never really understood what the Governor's Mansion is on Route 5 or why he never lived there.

- You might be from Oneida if you are stuck in traffic at 5PM on Route 5 and wait 5 minutes to move, while passersby from NYC laugh at you, saying, "You call this traffic?"

- You might be from Oneida if you actually did tip a cow or two as a rite of passage.

- You might be from Oneida if you decide to go out for a walk and ten people stop and ask you if you need a ride somewhere.

- You might be from Oneida if you accidentally call a wrong number and the person on the other end tells you the right number of the person you are looking for.

- You might be from Oneida if you believe "down South" is Cortland and "up North" is Old Forge.

- You might be from Oneida if you took the "mini brook" shortcut to school.

- You might be from Oneida if you played basketball at St. Joe's in the old gym.

- You might be from Oneida if you went to dances at St. Pat's and anxiously waited for "Freebird" or "Paradise by The Dashboard Lights" to be played at the end.

- You might be from Oneida if you remember live bands in Allen Park and everyone came out to dance.

- You might be from Oneida if you think Facebook is another word for "Photo Album."

- You might be from Oneida if you remember "The View" on Mount Hope as another term for Ritchie Cunningham's "Inspiration Point."

- You might be from Oneida if you roller-skated at the Kallet and let the girl go backwards because she could and you were too cool to let her know you couldn't.

- You might be from Oneida if you saw "Rocky" for the first time at the Oneida Cinema and everyone stood up and cheered when Apollo Creed said, "There ain't gonna be no rematch."

- You might be from Oneida if you call Italian food "macaroni" instead of "pasta."

- You might be from Oneida if you are not sure if when "The Hill" is mentioned, it might mean where the Y is, where the reservoir is, or where to get great wings on Friday night.

- You might be from Oneida if "Recovery" can mean either the morning after getting wings or the "new place by the casino."

- You might be from Oneida if you remember H.L. Green, IBC, the Dairy Parlor, Alfred's, Woolworth's, Carrols, Carl's, Fay's, Ames, FBC, Dandee Doughnuts, Grants, Lynn's, Gussie's, The Gin Mill, Dave's Market, Mrs. Grottle, Vic's, Agway, P&C, Bartell's, Joe Beer's, Miss Oneida Diner, and Friday's.

# Ten Items or Less

I usually go to the grocery store with a mission in mind. I know I need a bunch of stuff, but I'm a typical guy and forget to make a list, always thinking, "I know I need cucumbers and something else," hoping I'll remember it once I get in the door. I also have this crazy belief that real guys do not need a cart. Even more real guys don't need a basket. So, off I go into the produce aisle.

I am quickly sprayed by the automatic watering mechanism, as if I am going under Niagara Falls in the Maid of the Mist. Wet, I wrap my cucumbers in a baggie that I tear off the roller. It takes me several tries to find the end with the opening, discarding several of what I consider "faulty" bags. On to the cheese. I grab a port wine circle of "cheese food." I'm not really sure what "cheese food" is, but it is colorful, and goes well with processed crackers. I am now cradling the cucumbers like a baby in my right arm, while balancing the cheese on my elbow. I decide that I should have more fish in my diet and walk over to the meat and seafood cooler. What appears to be a large carp is staring at me through a glass window. Neither he nor I is eager to spend time with each other. The sign says "Pickerel," but I still think it's a carp. I feel the lobsters are laughing at me, and although I know that their claws are held together by rubber bands, I don't argue and make my way to the poultry section, grabbing some chicken parts. The chicken is held in the left hand. Other shoppers are passing by now offering, "Looks like you could use a cart." I smile and proceed, thinking to myself, "A cart? Real guys don't use carts!" The cucumbers fall on the floor and roll under a mom's cart that resembles a Volkswagen. Her little boy picks up the bag and throws it at me.

Suddenly, I remember what I came for – almonds. Because I forgot my glasses, I am straining to see the signs above the aisles to determine what is in each one. I don't see a sign that says "nuts," but I reason that they would be with baking stuff. The choice for almonds is overwhelming. There are chocolate-covered, wasabi, peanut butter, pepper, sea salt, and more. Too many for me, so I go with none – completely eliminating my need to be here. But since I've already committed to this shopping thing, and it would take too long to put things back, I press on.

The temperature changes drastically in the frozen food section. I was sweating coming in from the ninety-two degree heat, but now the perspiration is frozen to my forehead. The beer looks good in the section behind me, right behind the pickled beets. I have a suggestion for management – free samples. Beer, not beets, though.

I pass through the yogurt section, see the zillion choices and decide on blueberry, five of them. Even though there is a special, ten for ten dollars, I do not think I can eat ten and go with five. I stack these carefully along my forearm. I am now balanced. I am praying I do not have to sneeze (because I have caught a cold from the frozen sweat), and quickly walk past the baked goods section, as yet another shopper says, "You look like you could use a cart." I wince and sprint for the express counter, but the smell of the muffins directs my last remaining free fingers to grab a small bag of chocolate chip pastries. The pinky can come in handy. Looking up at the sign that states clearly "10 items or less," I throw down my 14 items and take a deep breath, feeling accomplished. The elderly lady in front of me suggests, "Here, take my cart...Please. Take my cart." I respond with, "No, I'm okay, thanks." She replies, "I'm not asking you; take the cart. And get out of the express lane."

I now have all of my bags in both hands, cutting off the circulation in my fingers and run to the car. Of course it is locked and I can't remember at first where I put my keys. They turn out to be in my front pocket but putting the bags down will cause imbalance. I carefully lay my groceries on the trunk, and unlock the door, while the cucumbers roll to the ground (for the second time) under the car. I'm sweating again. A cart would've been nice.

# Bible Study Part II

I would like to thank the many folks who have called, emailed, and visited me regarding my column about my Bible studies and progress. It's nice to know that I am not alone out there. And, to my new friends - thank you for reaching out to me. I was a little nervous how people might take it, but the response has been overwhelming. Shortly after the column appeared, I planned on going to mass that Sunday. I wasn't even sure what church I was going to. I was all set to go to a 10:30 AM service and decided to go to the Regional Market in Syracuse in the morning, hoping to be back in time. I went with my sister and a friend and got a little tied up. I was late and thought to myself, "Ugh, I really wanted to go, had the right intentions, but oh well, maybe I'll go next week." That sounds familiar. We had just gotten two or three inches of wet snow that morning and the roads were slick. After I dropped off my sister, I was driving home and out of the corner of my eye, I spotted an elderly lady with a walker trying to shovel her driveway. She was actually trying to push the shovel with her walker. The blade barely grazed the heavy snow.

I thought to myself, as I have done probably a thousand times, "Ah, I'm sure she's got someone to help her" and drove on. I got home, put my hands on my hips and sighed, grabbed my shovel out of the garage, and drove back down the street. Parking on the side of the road, I walked to her driveway and just started shoveling. She stopped me and said, "Oh, you must have heard me," in a whispery, sweet tone. I wasn't sure she was talking to me because she was kind of looking around me. I said, "Excuse me?" and she said,

"I was just praying someone would come and help me and here you are." Then, she said, "How old are you?" I replied, "I'm 47," and she said, "I'm 84." We shook hands without even exchanging names. I said, "How about if you go inside and stay warm; I've got this." She asked me to write my name down so that she could give me some money. I said, "That's not necessary; I'm the thankful one." I finished the whole driveway and went and got her mail and newspaper for her and brought them to the front door. Walking away to my car, I turned back and saw that she was looking out the doorway. I said to myself quietly, "Thank you, ma'am."

I've mentioned before I don't believe in luck or coincidence anymore and this was another example. I've driven by many people who probably needed help. I've turned the other way a bunch of times. I've been on the Thruway going by cars that are broken down and thought, "I'm sure someone is on their way to help them." Today was different. I also know that there are hundreds of people, especially in our community, who would have helped her too. My mom and dad always taught me to help others when they need it. And it wasn't a big deal. Part of growing is paying attention. I got back in the car and on my CD player was my Beatles "Number Ones" CD: *"There's nothing you can know that isn't known. Nothing you can see that can't be shown. Nowhere you can be that isn't where you're meant to be. It's easy…"*

Coincidence? I doubt it.

# The Song That Changed My World

Several years ago, when I was working on our YMCA recording project that featured young music students recording with national recording artists, I was referred to Denise Morgan, the lead singer from the Marvelettes. I called Denise and introduced myself and told her what we were doing and asked if she would be interested and if she had a song. She said she had a tune she had written 29 years earlier called "Where Are They," but had never recorded it. She sent it to me on an old, scratchy cassette. I didn't even have a player, so had it converted to a CD. After listening to the lyrics, I was floored. I thought, "Wow, this is from a mom to a child; what a powerful song." I immediately called Denise and asked for her permission to contact the National Center for Missing & Exploited Children and share it. She agreed. I called the Community Foundation and asked if they had a contact and it just so happened Kelly Corasanti, who was on the committee, was in their office. I scheduled an appointment and brought the song and played it for them. We all cried.

*"Where are they?*
*I shed a tear tonight*
*Peacefully sleeping*
*Or living in fright*
*Where are the children?*
*Please bring the children back home"*

(Denise Morgan. "Where are They." *Hope is in Me: A Musical Journey.* YCCA Collaborations III: Hope, 2003.)

It was my introduction to NCMEC and all of the great work they do. We then started to partner with them on training for YMCA staff on abduction prevention and safety. That year, Denise performed "Where Are They" with YMCA kids to a packed New Hartford Recreation Center of 2,000 at the closing ceremonies of the Ride for Missing Children. With thousands of lit candles in a darkened room, there wasn't a dry eye. Denise barely made it through the song. Two years later, and after many trainings, ceremonies, and more, the NYS Troop D Barracks was under construction and the Ride For Missing Children needed a home for the Opening Ceremonies. I offered the Y and they were very thankful. At our first planning meeting, someone from NCMEC, asked, "Hey Hank, why don't you ride with us?" Having not ridden a bike since it had three wheels, I said…"Um, er, okay." I trained, lost thirty pounds, recruited the local school district superintendent, and we completed the 100-mile journey to raise money for posters of missing children.

This year, I am riding in my second Ride. Many Oneida teachers are joining us, as well as two YMCA board members and two school board members. As the 500 cyclists, family members of missing children, supporters, law enforcement, and public send us off, I will again sit in amazement. We currently work together to train hundreds of staff in child abuse prevention, offer workshops to educators, parents and kids, and the CD/DVD "Hope Is In Me," that features "Where Are They" was nominated for a Feel Good Film Festival Award in Hollywood last year. I am in the process of working on funding to re-record a song called "Bells of Love," written in 1993 for Sara Anne Wood, a victim of child abduction, by a music educator in Syracuse. We are going to try to re-record the song in "We Are the World" fashion with national recording artists from around the world as a music download to raise funds for posters.

The power of one song is indescribable. The impact it has is everlasting. If one song brings home one lost child, it is all worth it.

# Readin', 'Riting, and Ramen Noodles

Those who go away to college understand that this is the four-year period of life where you go from being a teenager to an adult, and very quickly. When you first head off to school, it is bittersweet. Some can't wait to get away from their childhood home to go and meet new friends, learn a new city, experience life, and take on the world. Others are skeptical, wanting to stay close to home, near the comfort of Mom and Dad. I ended up somewhere in the middle. When I went to college, I was excited, nervous, and ready to go. In usual Leo fashion, I arrived at school about a week early, for no particular reason. They were training Resident Assistants and performing pre-orientations. Because I was there so early, and one of the "RAs" had to opt out, I was asked to serve as an alternate. I agreed. Free room and half board were enticing to an 18-year old with an annual income of zero.

The four-year period of higher education is not just made up of books and professors. I learned through trial and error how to wash and dry clothes in a dirty basement, iron on the floor, stay up twenty-four hours straight, make Ramen Noodles on a hot plate, navigate through unmarked buildings for classes with three hundred other students, and find out that Astronomy is not a "blow-off" class. In fact, I thought Astronomy was going to be easy and fulfill my elective requirement. I probably should have looked a little more closely at the course description. When, on the second day of class, the professor stated casually, "Today, we are going to calculate the mass of the universe," it should have been an alert of things to come. My friend John and I squinted disbelievingly through a telescope on top of the academic building, looking at a bright light flashing through the sky. We asked, "Wow, professor, is that one of the moons of Jupiter?" The good doctor replied, "No, that's not Jupiter; that's the Cortland airport."

In the mid-'80s, college was fun. I met hundreds of new friends, learned that classes were going to be tough, and that dating was going to be even tougher. Try taking a girl out with $1.68 in change. I think I bought her a card and we went hiking. And yes, the hike was in the cemetery on Halloween, but nonetheless, a hike.

I had a car, but never any gas. Road trips were awesome and only occurred when we pooled our change to chip in for gas. This didn't get us very far. Most often, our road trips turned out to be a weekend trip home for some of my mom's cooking. All of my friends came to love her cooking, too. I remember one time, waking up in my dorm room on a Sunday at mid-morning, and my roommate nowhere to be found. I called home to say hi to Mom and when the phone rang, my roommate picked up the phone. I thought I was having a dream. "What are you doing at my house?" I demanded. He responded, "Having a homemade omelet with your mom."

When I look back on my college days, it seems like such a short period of time, like it flew by. It was only four years long, but it was four of the best years of my life. Going from a nervous kid in a small town, into college life with thousands of other nervous kids, to a young adult, pretty much overnight, had an overwhelming affect on me. It was a crash course in adulthood.

# Labor Day Revelations

1. It rains way too much here.
2. I have 150 channels and can't find anything to watch.
3. Baseball lasts much too long and should be done in August, even the Yankees.
4. I'm never really sure when the NFL real season begins and the pre-season is over.
5. Even though everyone says they hate the State Fair, everyone goes, has a great time, then goes again.
6. I mow the lawn every other day.
7. My dog is secretly plotting against me.
8. I have no idea why I wash my car; it seems pointless.
9. Facebook is a good thing; a few idiots give it a bad name.
10. School starting reminds me of No. 2 pencils.
11. I need to get in better shape if I'm going to hibernate again this winter.
12. Ronnie Dunn doesn't need Kix Brooks; Steve Perry doesn't need Journey, and Foreigner needs Lou Gramm.
13. September 11th seemed like yesterday and still makes me mad, sad, and proud all at the same time.
14. The truth is often forgotten because of poor perceptions.
15. I hate snowblowers, scrapers, salt, shovels, roof rakes, boots, gloves, and the rest.
16. I am still learning texting abbreviations, LOL.
17. Hearing the evils of root canals, they are true - when I chew, I can feel it in my feet.

18. I need to go to church more often, even though I pray every day.
19. The Hops Fest is coming up; I usually volunteer to pour, but end up sampling.
20. I should read more often.
21. Everything that comes from my dad's garden tastes a little better than anything else.
22. The Mets need my managerial skills.
23. I am going to take harmonica, swimming, and cooking lessons this fall, maybe even in the same day.
24. I hate ironing and it shows.
25. I'm wondering why I have the day off on Labor Day.

# The Post Office

Most of the time, I only have to go to a post office to send in a credit card payment and I do so by putting the letter into the drive-up box. I'm not clear why there are always two mailboxes. I don't see the difference in them and they are always right next to each other. I usually select the one on the left, only because I am left-handed, and it feels like that is the right one. I have no idea why; I have been doing it for years, and have never asked. I am sure there is a logical explanation. It might have something to do with two different pick-up times, but I'm not sure why they either don't pick them both up at the same time or have one box with two times. Maybe one of the openings is larger; again, I am not sure. I'm usually just happy that my mirror or my elbow didn't hit the box this time.

On this particular day, however, I realized that I didn't have a stamp on my envelope and needed to go inside. Why is it that no matter which side of the street you want to park on, there is always a line of cars on that side while the other side is empty? Then, you have to make that decision whether or not to circle the block, risking that the empty side will then be full while the one you are currently on can quickly become evacuated. I decided to perform the possibly illegal "U-ey" and select the one directly across the street. Ah, it was going to be a good day.

As I approach the door, I want to be a good citizen and hold the door for folks, but today I realize I am most likely adding to what I am sure is a line already forming from the counter to the boxes. The elderly man I let in says, "Thanks, Bub." I wince and wonder if I am in line for Springsteen tickets and look to see if I have a "Bub" nametag on. As I enter the lobby there is that imaginary line that you don't cross, waiting until it's your turn. There's not much to look at in the lobby other than examples of box sizes and the coin-operated copy machine, and no one talks to each other, like in an elevator. I've been to small post offices in rural areas - you know the kind - where there is a paper clock on the door that reads "Be back at 1:00." You look at your watch and it is 1:10 and the door is still locked with no one to be found. "Had to turn off the crock-pot," is the response. It doesn't really matter what time or day I go to the post office. The man in front of me inevitably will have a package that he wrapped himself in a paper bag, duct-taping the corners, and it will read, "To Bobby, From Mike...United Kingdom." I already anticipate impatience. I only need one stamp.

The line moves slowly, and I mean slowly. It may have something to do with the lady who needs to insure her triangular cardboard contraption. I can only guess it is an oversized billiards rack. The man in front of me proceeds to the window. "Sir, do you have a return address for this package to Europe?" asks the attendant. "Uh, nope," is the reply. "Not gonna be livin' here when this gets there; if it gets there at all. My buddy's in England and he needs this. You guys lost my last one," he exclaims. "Well, maybe if you provided an..." she starts to reason. She then collects herself. "Do you want to insure this? Delivery confirmation?" she offers. "Insure a pie?" he responds slightly agitated. I get nervous there is going to be an incident, and understand now what "going postal" is all about. In fact, I am thinking of defending the attendant's honor as the man moves on, mumbling about finding some sort of zip code for the United Kingdom. He shakes the pen, which is dangling from a broken chain, complaining that it is out of ink.

It is my turn. "One stamp, please," I proclaim rather calmly. "Do you want flowers or Eiffel Tower?" is the response. I am really not sure I understand the question, or its validity. But I like both flowers and France (even though they don't like us), and say, "Flowers, please." I am not even all that confident that it matters what kind of stamp I buy. I am the one sending the stamp, not receiving it. But, it is a sunny day out, flowers are nice things, and I feel that maybe the recipient would be happy to get flowers, albeit in sticky, paper form that will end up in a shredder. She tears off a corner of a stamp book with one of the flower stamps on it. I cannot recall how much stamps cost. I think to myself as I toss out $.40, "I think they were $.02 a little while ago, but they might be $.50 now, hmm." I do recall however that there are things called "Forever" stamps, but I think they are called that only because it describes the length of the line in any post office. Affixing my new bouquet of flowers on my envelope, I realize I am sending a nice little slice of my day to a credit card company, at a PO Box in Wilmington, Delaware. I would hate to see the size of that PO Box. My guess is the recipient is a machine, or robot of some sort, that couldn't care less about flowers and probably would have appreciated the Eiffel Tower stamp instead.

As I lick the envelope, I lose all desire for dinner, and drop it into the slot. Another customer in line asks the attendant, "How big of a box do you think I need to send myself a fruit cake? How long will it take to get to Florida? I am driving to Naples tonight and want to make sure I'm there when it gets there." To all of the post office workers: you have my greatest respect and sympathy. Keep that smile despite the lines, crazy questions, and impatience.

# Ride of My Life

As the middle of May dawns, I am saddling a road bike, just about ready to leave for my second Ride For Missing Children, the 100-mile journey to bring awareness to, and raise funds for, posters that help find missing children. This has become a passion of mine and one that means a lot to me both on a personal and professional level. For the past several months, I've been training hard to get in shape.

The Ride is a physical challenge as we need to complete the journey which starts at the Oneida YMCA and weaves through the Mohawk Valley, ending twelve hours later at the New Hartford Recreation Center. If you've seen the seats we sit on, you know they just weren't built for guys. I equate the experience to balancing on a railing. Thank God the Ride stops on five occasions to visit schools and cheering kids who support the cause.

The event is also an emotional one. We are always told that if we ever feel tired, nervous, scared, or unsure that we can continue, to think of the families who are missing a child. Riding a bike is nowhere near the mountain of anguish that a family goes through during and after an abduction. I have heard family members speak, and have ridden with those who have not yet found their child. My complaints about the comfort of a bike seat go away very quickly. Last year was my first time riding, and I am not a cyclist by any means. I didn't have a bike, and I didn't know the whole process. I simply knew, as I sat in the audience at the opening and closing ceremonies, that I was doing something special for someone. Each rider rides for a particular child and displays their photo proudly on their jersey. The jerseys are colored pink and turquoise, the colors Sarah Anne Wood wore when she was abducted. Last year I rode for a young man from Cazenovia who was killed in 1992. I had met him briefly when I worked in Cazenovia at the Eidos Program and he was a great kid. Along the Ride, at one of the stops, I met his mom and we shared a hug and tears.

This year, I am a little more seasoned and know what to expect. I keep myself focused on the cause, the families, the purpose. When I say to myself, "I don't feel like riding today, I'm a little tired," I remind myself that a dad who is missing a child would never say, "I don't feel like looking for my son today." The aches and pains go away. The smile returns. My legs feel like working. I have a little prayer I like to say when I am not sure when or who to help; it is in Peter 4:10. "As each has received a gift, use it to serve one another, as good stewards of God's varied grace."

I guess my gift is that I am physically able to ride a bike 100 miles. I could do it for fun, but I'd rather do it to help someone. To all of the five hundred riders and friends, it is an honor to be a part of such a moving and important event. Wind at our backs, let's bring some children home.

# Remember Your First Car?

Who doesn't…I had a 'Vet. No, not a Corvette, a Chev-ette. It was masculine neon-green and there were no floorboards. In fact, one time while I was driving, something underneath caught on fire. I am not sure what caused it and I don't even remember how I put it out. I do remember, however, that it had a killer stereo. No, Chevy did not install incredible sound systems in their Chevettes in the late '70s. I really didn't care what the car looked like, how fast it went, or how many seats it had. If it held two bookshelf speakers in the back, with red speaker wire running the length of the car, it was fine.

I remember springing for the tape deck model. I really wanted the "new fangled one" that when the tape got to the end on the first side, it automatically started playing the backside. You were also able to fast forward the tape as it mysteriously located the gap between songs. Unfortunately, I couldn't afford that one, so just the regular tape deck had to suffice. I found it absolutely necessary that despite the potential for the car to catch on fire, it had to be able to play "Back in Black" at a level where the rearview mirror vibrated. After a short time, I "donated" the car to my little sister.

My next car was a convertible blue Dodge Shadow. I thought that having a convertible meant something very special. What I discovered was two distinct truths: people with convertibles get wet before everyone else, and you get asked to drive old boxing stars in the International Boxing Hall of Fame Parade annually. The top to my Shadow never seemed to really fit the car. I don't know if it shrunk or the car grew - I just know that tugging and pulling on one of the corners to batten down the hatches during a rainstorm on the Thruway was both a lesson in humility and an Olympic event. I remember driving the Great White Hope, Jerry Quarry, down Peterboro Street in June in my Dodge Shadow, and it was a session of prayer. I do not recall how many times I actually said, "God, please let the car start; don't let Mr. Quarry fall between my seats; and if we hit a bump, by all means - make him stay in the car."

I am also a self-proclaimed deer magnet. I have hit a total of eight deer in my life; the most notable was five miles from the dealership in Buffalo with a new Chevy Beretta. Yes, that was five miles on the odometer. Shortly after "the incident," I purchased deer whistlers, or "deer alerts" designed to, I guess, send out some micro-supersonic-pitch that no one can hear other than deer, letting them know a car was approaching. I imagine this just confused them. It confused me, as well. With my Beretta fully-repaired and ready to roll weeks later, I struck deer number two. I recall pulling deer hair out of the deer whistlers, and saying to the trooper, "I have some deer alerts I'd like to sell you, along with some beachfront property in Wampsville." He did not laugh; instead he suggested hunters take me with them as a lure.

There were a number of other vehicles in my crazy car history including a Subaru something (I don't think it had a model), a Toyota Corolla that was great on gas but couldn't make it up Tilden Hill, and a Datsun blah, blah, blah with a "12" on it. It ran when I pushed it. It didn't when I was tired.

I am very happy now with my Honda Accord, though the antenna fell off in last year's snowstorm. I can only get WMCR, our local radio station, I only hear every third word from the DJ and it sounds like I am always going under a bridge. I like the new WMCR format and get to hear most of the words Joel Meltzer reports. When I am on Route 5 headed to the Y, I get to hear the whole report. Thank goodness for my iPod when I reach the signal limit.

# Words of Wisdom from Dr. Seuss

I was one of those kids who loved Dr. Seuss and still do. I've read every book Mr. Geisel wrote, including his autobiography, and I refer to them many times in speeches I give. As absurd, tongue-twisting, and confusing as the books can be to many people, young and old, I always saw them as hidden messages about accepting others despite their differences. For a few years, my good friends Carolyn Gerakopoulos and Michelle Ryan at the Oneida Library would ask me to dress up as the Cat in the Hat himself and read to the little ones. I always chose *Sneeches*, one of my all time favorites. There is a semi-famous Oneida Dispatch photo of me in costume, bending over a toddler, who is looking up at me, scared to death of an 8-foot giant cat. I think I also scared Morris Atwood, the Adult Literacy Coordinator and a former teacher of mine. Anyway…here are a few quotes from my favorite Dr. Seuss books and what they mean to me:

- *"When the Star-Belly children went out to play ball, Could a Plain Belly get in the game? Not at all. You only could play if your bellies had stars. And the Plain-Belly children had none upon thars"* [Taken from: Dr. Seuss (1961). *The Sneetches and Other Stories.* New York: Random House.]

  Translation: Every kid who didn't fit in feels this way. It's just ridiculous to not have everyone participate regardless of their age, race, ability, income level, or physique.

- *"The more things you read, the more things you'll know. The more that you learn, the more places you'll go"* [Taken from: Dr. Seuss

(1978). *I Can Read with My Eyes Shut!* New York: Random House Books for Young Readers; First Edition.]

Translation: Everyone should read; it expands your vocabulary, your intelligence, and your world.

- *"My alphabet starts with this letter called yuzz. It's the letter I use to spell yuzz-a-matuzz. You'll be sort of surprised what there is to be found once you go beyond 'Z' and start poking around!"* [Taken from: Dr. Seuss (1963). *Dr. Seuss's ABC.* New York: Random House Beginner Books; First Edition.]

Translation: Think outside the box; be creative and go beyond what is expected of you. Don't be afraid to think differently.

- *"Be who you are and say what you feel because those who mind don't matter and those who matter don't mind."* [Taken from: Dr. Seuss (1990). *Oh, the Places You'll Go!* New York: Random House.]

Translation: Be honest and true to yourself even though some people might not like what you have to say; those who matter to you will respect you.

- *"From there to here, from here to there, funny things are everywhere."* [Taken from: Dr. Seuss (1960). *One Fish Two Fish Red Fish Blue Fish.* New York: Random House Books for Young Readers.]

Translation: As serious as life can sometimes get, never lose your sense of humor.

- *"Young cat, if you keep your eyes open enough, oh, the stuff you would learn! The most wonderful stuff!"* [Taken from: Dr. Seuss (1997). *Seuss-isms: Wise and Witty Prescriptions for Living from the Good Doctor.* New York: Random House Books for Young Readers.]

Translation: Don't go through life watching it pass you by. Be awake and a part of your thoughts and be aware of others and how they feel.

- And my personal favorite: *"When beetles fight these battles in a bottle with their paddles and the bottle's on a poodle and the poodle's eating noodles......they call this a muddle puddle tweetle poodle beetle noodle bottle paddle battle."* [Taken from: Dr. Seuss (1965). *Fox in Socks.* New York: Random House Books for Young Readers.]

Translation: I have no idea, but it makes me smile.

Ted Geisel used to say, "I like non-sense. It wakes up the brain cells." It's easy to go through life and simply get old. Time flies by. One day we are graduating from high school and the next we are going to our thirty-year reunion. Over the past few years, I have come to the conclusion that we are born and we die. What happens after that depends on what you did in-between. So, here's a quote of my own, in Seussism fashion:

*You just never know what today will bring, or tomorrow or 257 Tuesdays Or anything.*

*What you do from this Tuesday to 256 can be much more than darts, hop-scotch or pick-up-sticks.*

*Be good to others all of the days; you do the work, and let them count the ways.*

# Friendship

We go through our trials and tribulations with friends over the years. Every day I see people that I went to elementary school with and who live in my town, yet I've never invited them to my house or been invited to theirs. On the other hand, I've gone to dinner and a movie with people I met just last week. I think sometimes we search for people we can connect with. The connection is what makes or breaks a friendship. That is followed by trust, honesty, and understanding. I have heard people define friendship on several occasions. "A true friend is someone who's got your back, no matter what." "A friend is someone who loves me for who I am." "A friend is a guy who'd give you the shirt off his back." "My best friend is my brother from another mother." Or, "She is always there for me."

It seems that the common thread is what the other person would do for you, no matter the circumstances. It's rare to hear the comment, "A true friend will tell you when you are screwing up." Or, "A real friend wouldn't make excuses for you. She would hold you accountable." Now we all know that a true friend is the one who will help you move from one house to another and pay you with pizza and beer. They will supervise while you get the washing machine from the basement. "I'm gonna go pick up the pizza. Can you grab the bed from the master bedroom and bring it down the spiral staircase? I'll be right back." Upon returning, your friend is lying on his back with the mattress covering him, moaning something resembling, "Help ... beer ... help ... beer." A true friend.

Friends also share your perspective and don't disagree with you when you are on a rant, or just need to vent. "Man, the price of gas is terrible! There isn't even a shortage! The oil companies are just greedy and we pay for it!" Your true friend responds, "I'll get the chips; it's gonna be a long drive. Want anything?" No argument. Friends also feel free to change the radio station in your car:

"What is this crap you're listening to?"

"Hey, leave that. You don't like country? Are you kidding?"

"I remember when you didn't like country, either. When did you become a twang?"

"My friend's brother turned me on to it. I can't take Ozzy Osborne anymore. Hurts my ears. Plus, have you seen his show?"

"It's awesome. Love the Osbornes."

Then we move on. Agree to disagree. We can live with Kenny Chesney and Ozzy. And, they might even perform together on "Crossroads," so we can both be happy.

Friends use peer pressure, even at my age. "Hey, you look pretty good in a pink button down." The next day, I am shopping for a new shirt in the metrosexual section of the men's clothing section.

"Looks like you haven't missed too many meals lately." The next day he's eating a rice cake and yogurt.

Then there is the danger of women friends getting together without the guys, and the guys getting together without their spouses. At "girls night out," women use wine as fuel to gain perspective on the universe. They solve the world's problems, figure out how simple men are, and learn that they really do not need them in their lives. As long as they have wine and each other, there is no need for the opposite sex. If a bunch of guys got together and had wine, they'd probably be crying and calling their wives or girlfriends, telling them they miss them, and asking them to pick them up, apologizing for being away for so long. That's why someone invented football. The game takes the place of drinking wine with friends and getting introspective.

Guy friends talk about very little and certainly nothing of substance. We'd rather do stuff. We like to golf, watch a game, and eat. The only time we talk about women is when we have problems, then good friends offer the couch. Peripheral friends wish you luck. Guys also know sports statistics, including batting averages, yards per carry, records, and the standings. And guys know how many points Kobe had last night. We know what a double double is, a grand salami, a hat trick, a suicide squeeze, and offensive interference. Guy friends can also quote movie lines from any comedy. *Caddyshack* is filled with them and any guy worth his salt knows all of them.

I think women talk about pretty much everything and nothing is off limits. The topics range from shoes, to purses, to relationships, to books, to movies and to love. They can go through bottle after bottle of Red Cat, while crying, laughing, eating, and talking about horoscopes. Little things make a big difference. "It's not what he said, but how he said it." Girlfriends rally together and form a bond that is stronger than Superglue. Guys are weak, scared, and melt in the face of this teamwork. If you want to see a he-man turn into a puddle of mush, simply let him know his girl just called and wants to know when he's coming home. Strong as an ox at first, followed quickly by jellyfish.

At the end of an evening, everyone goes home affirming that although they had fun, they would have had a better time if had they been with each other. The women interrogate the men on who said what, which is an act of futility since the men didn't talk about anything and if they had, they wouldn't remember. One of the women usually suggests they all get together next time to watch *The Notebook*, and the men all say, "Sure." This, too, will, and should, be forgotten.

# Baseball Cards

I've been collecting baseball cards ever since I was five or six years old. I made the classic mistakes, though. Yes, I put the best ones in my bike spokes to hear the flapping sound as I peddled my way to a friend's house, only to learn forty years later that the card, in excellent condition, would be worth hundreds. I also grew up a New York Mets fan in a world where the Yankees were king. I thought very logically that getting a Cleon Jones card in return for my 1955 Mickey Mantle was a steal. Little did I know that the world would treasure Mantle, and Jones would fall into relative obscurity. I also used to write on the ones I really liked. Something to the effect of "good one," labeled the guy that I thought was going somewhere. A ten-year-old's hand-scripted ink rendition of support doesn't carry any weight with the card graders, apparently.

I couldn't stand Babe Ruth and had one of his cards. I think I turned it into a miniature paper airplane and sailed it out of my second floor bedroom window in front of an oncoming truck. I looked up that card recently and found it to be worth in excess of $1,500. But my 1977 Doug Flynn card is in pristine shape, carefully placed inside a plastic protector. The corners are razor sharp and the picture is centered perfectly. It goes now for just under $.25 on eBay.

Cards are still being collected today and I still buy a pack or two when I am at the store. They have changed a lot. They actually put a piece of a uniform from a player inside the card. These are called "Game-used jersey cards." They also have "Game-used pants cards" and "Game-used helmet" cards. No one knows for sure whether these are actually pieces of jerseys, pants, or helmets, and I am not sure I want someone's game-used pants. If you know ballplayers... oh well.

The other interesting fact is that cards that are made now, of a guy like Bryce Harper, the 19-year old phenom from Washington, are worth more than, let's say, Johnny Bench. The kids today know Bryce Harper. They think Johnny Bench is where their grandfather keeps the yard tools. It's quite a shame. Baseball players change teams so often now that there are twelve cards of a guy with twelve different uniforms on in twelve different years. Keeping track of where the guy played is not an easy task.

I now have somewhere around ten thousand cards. They are not in any kind of order and I don't know who I have. They might be worth something some day, I am sure. But for now, I just like to have them. They remind me of my childhood, and I can even look at the card and remember where I was during that period. I can remember the grade, who my friends were, where my family was, and what I was doing. Baseball cards are like life's bookmarks.

# The Vegetable Garden

Growing up, my dad always had a vegetable garden. He would plant tomatoes, cucumbers, radishes, beans, carrots, and zucchini. As I became an adult, I would always stop over to Dad's house and pick up homemade sauce, fruits, and veggies. His garden was always perfect. Gigantic tomato plants, huge beans, gorgeous zucchini. This winter, I said to my dad, "I'd like to plant a garden this year." He looked at me like my head was a butternut squash. Now the Leos come from a long line of managers, take-charge guys, organizers, and delegators. We can't fix anything, but we are good at asking others to help us. I remember one time someone telling me they changed a spark plug in their lawn mower and I couldn't believe it was possible; I thought that is why we hire mechanics. Anyway, Leos are good at gardening. If the rototiller stops rototilling though, it is best for us to contact a professional.

So I asked Dad for the first step and he said, "Where do you want to put it?" I responded, "Behind the garage seems like a good place, no?" He said, "Well, if that's where you want it." But there was a question mark in his voice. I was bound and determined to have my own garden and stood my ground, but wondered why my choice of location was up for debate. "Yup, that's where I want it...I think, I guess, that is, if you think... Why? Is there something wrong with behind the garden?" We moved on.

My dad explained that his friend Pat had some "horse crap" that is good for the soil. He also explained that my dirt is terrible, "like clay." I didn't take it personally, but had no way of disagreeing. I didn't even know why clay was bad, and was afraid to ask. He kept looking at me with those eyes that are in his photograph on the living room wall of our family's house. You know, the kind where they follow you around.

The next day, I dug a hole with a shovel. Yes, it might have been a good idea to measure it out into some form of a shape. I apparently chose a triangle. I spent several hours, shoveling pile after pile of lawn. Just then Pat pulled up to my house in his big truck and dumped a huge load of fertilizer right behind my garage. "Here you go," he said with a smile. My dog ran through it, and urinated on what he considered the center. Pat added, "Maybe you should've used a turf lifter - a lot easier, you know." Three quarters of the way through this back-breaking process and now he tells me that someone had invented a tool that scrapes off the layer of grass easily. I responded, "Yeah, I could have, but I needed the workout; wanted to do it the old-fashioned way."

Pat left, saying, "Good luck, Hank. Who's going to pull the weeds?" I thought after you dug the hole, got rid of everything but the dirt, and put piles of horse poop on it, there wouldn't be weeds. After about a week, I could have mowed my garden, that's how bad it was.

I decided to plant peppers: hot peppers, sweet peppers, orange ones, red ones, green ones, and yellow ones. Heck, I would've planted blue ones if they had them. A neighbor politely informed me that we had deer and rabbits galore and I should probably put up a fence. Another "advisor" told me the best thing to do would be to put dog hair in the garden to keep rodents away. I have a Siberian Husky who is now completely shaved and little tufts of hair are threaded in and out of a one-foot fence. I'm pretty sure this fence won't even stop a mole.

I have no idea if these plants will take root, whether or not things will sprout, or if I've just been tricked into creating a horse poop museum. When I see my first pepper, I am having some sort of a celebration - maybe a Pepperfest. If not, I am hiring someone to build a garden for me. Or, better yet, peppers are on sale at the grocery store this week for $1.59 a pound; I'll be in the produce aisle if anyone needs me.

# The Dentist Office

I look around the waiting room while I sit perched on the wooden chair, agonizing over the moments to come. Brochures graphically describe the danger of gum disease, while subliminal warnings of gingivitis appear mystically in ads for Sonicare - which can brush my teeth 31,000 times in a minute. I am nervous and I don't want to be next. "Mr. Leo?" Ugh. "He left," is my response. They know better. "Follow me and the doctor will be right with you."

I recline in the chair and a paper napkin is attached to my collar. My mouth is already dry with nervousness. The hygienist comes in and far too casually comments, "You haven't been here in a while, have you?" I begin to panic. *"How does she know that? Do I have bad breath? Is it Gingivitis? How much does it say about me in that file, anyway?"* All of these thoughts run through my head. *"Maybe it's the broken tooth,"* I reason. *"Maybe it's the deformed molar in the back that cuts into my cheek when I smile,"* is what I settle on.

"I see you missed your last appointment," she states as she looks at my folder. I am relieved, but only for a second. "Open up wide for me," she urges. I panic again, lean back with my mouth open the size of a golf ball. She says, "Wider please!" I am afraid. Begrudgingly, I do as I am told. It is now the size of a softball, the same size as the lump in my throat.

She takes out a series of instruments. They look like the ones used in the Frankenstein movies. There is a cleaver, a machete, a few scissors, some scraping things, a couple of pink swabs, and a series of needles. I was hoping for the vibrating toothbrush, but to no avail. I try to make small talk. "How long have you been working here?" I ask. My internal voice is really asking, *What in God's name are those things and what do you intend to do with them? I haven't done anything to you!*" She responds, "Thirteen years." To me, this just means she has been torturing people for thirteen years. But she has the upper hand, so I let it go.

She then puts a large plastic something in my jaw and tells me to bite down. I feel as if it will cut my tongue off, but comply, wondering what it would really be like if I couldn't talk anymore. I then see what looks like a cave with stalagmites on a small television screen. She explains it is my X-ray. "I knew that," is my clever response.

The doctor arrives and we review my attendance again. "Good to see you Hank; it's been a while." Here we go. I start shaking and squirming. He informs me there is going to be "a little sting" and injects me using a 20 inch needle. I gasp to talk, but it comes out in a drool. I can't swallow. I don't know where to look.

A thin vacuum cleaner is then inserted into my mouth and it sucks up the side of my cheek and half my tongue. I spit in a swirly little toilet bowl and become dizzy. He reminds me not to bite down until the Novocain has worn off. I am now more afraid than when I walked in. I am reminiscing about the "hysterics" of laughing gas when I was a kid and wish I had some right now. "You have some pretty prehistoric dentistry in here," he shares. Not understanding, I respond, "Well, I am getting old." We move on. There are a lot of humming noises, smoke is coming out of my mouth, water droplets are shooting high enough to hit his protective glasses, and I smell burnt wood. I look up and am blinded by the spotlight on the guy with the miner's hat, who claims to be a dentist. I start praying and asking God if this is a sign. God responds, "No, you fool, quit being a wimp and let the guy finish, will you?"

As I leave, I thank the folks for sparing my life. An older lady is coming in as I am leaving, and says, "How are you?" I respond, "Hewoah...dis nobicane is pwetty good stupff." She points to my tie, where there is a newly-formed wet spot and motions for me to dry off my chin. I say, "Sorwy. I ma mess. I been tru heow in heow and I..." She responds with "Bite your tongue!" And I oblige.

# What's Not Exciting About an Average Day in the Life?

I often get asked how I came up with things to write about for a weekly column. I always say there is plenty of material out there. We sometimes get caught up in the media, hearing about extremes in life and the little stuff gets buried. It's what draws attention that gets the headlines. I've always found normal, daily life to be enough to worry about, not caring very much whether Tom Cruise and Katie Holmes are taking a break from their relationship or where the super-rich are vacationing. I think sometimes we call our lives boring when we go on a vacation, walk our dog, go to the movies, shop at a grocery store, or buy a stamp at the post office. Whether you live in a big city or small town, we all do pretty much the same things: wake up, go to work or school, go home, eat, have family and friend time, and go to bed. Writing this book has taught me many things. Sometimes it felt like I was standing still and thousands of things were happening all around me. Recording my thoughts helped me to pay attention. Much of what I observed affected me more than I thought it would, but the truth is that before I knew it, years had passed by. As a friend once said, "Long days, short years."

It wasn't until a couple of years ago that I came to the realization that I'd like to have a lever that stops everything exactly when I'd like it to. Sometimes when I write, it's about a particular moment when I pulled that imaginary lever and looked around me. I know that nothing has really stopped, but I feel like I'm seeing things from a different angle, rather than going through the motions. It has helped in a lot of ways. Holding the door open for someone takes on a new meaning. So does going fishing with my dad. A few years ago, I would worry whether or not it was going to rain, what time we would get done, if I would catch anything except a cold. Now, I remember the look of gratitude from the elderly lady at the door, and the smile on my dad's face when we came to shore, talking about all of the big ones that got away.

Daily living. It's hard. It's also filled with surprises, things that make me laugh, things that make me cry. It reminds me of something my friend Jason Marsalis, the famous drummer from the musical Marsalis family, told me. When his dad Ellis was asked why he only plays the piano, Ellis, one of the premiere jazz pianists of all time responded, "Playing the piano is hard enough; I'm struggling just trying to do that." Nothing big has to happen for us to understand that simple and routine are exciting enough. Many of my stories are memories of the little things, daily routine stuff, with a few sprinkles of special moments that decorate the life of an average guy. Most times, people kind of let them drift by, as passing snippets of time. I like to write about them.

Tonight I may just drive home by way of Allen Park. In fact, I may just pull over and watch the kids playing Kick- the-Can or tag. I'll look over my shoulder and see my mom and dad's house, and look up to that second floor room. I'll remember staring out that bedroom window as a kid, eagerly waiting for the next day, and the next adventure. And sure enough, I'll head home when the streetlights come on.